LET'S GO FISHING!

© Roger Preuss

Let's Go Fishing!

Fish Tales from the NORTH WOODS

 Eric Dregni

University of Minnesota Press

Minneapolis • London

The University of Minnesota Press gratefully acknowledges the generous assistance provided for the publication of this book by the Hamilton P. Traub University Press Fund.

Frontispiece: Roger Preuss, *End of a Perfect Day,* circa 1945. Watercolor, 14 × 18 inches. Courtesy of the Minnesota Historical Society.

Recipe for Lynne Rossetto Kasper's Sweet/Sour Ice House Fish Stew copyright 2010 Lynne Rossetto Kasper, host, *The Splendid Table*®, American Public Media, Minnesota Public Radio.

Published by the University of Minnesota Press
111 Third Avenue South, Suite 290
Minneapolis, MN 55401-2520
http://www.upress.umn.edu

Design and production by Mighty Media, Inc.
Interior and text design by Chris Long

ISBN 978-0-8166-9321-4

A Cataloging-in-Publication record for this title is available from the Library of Congress.

Printed in China on acid-free paper

The University of Minnesota is an equal-opportunity educator and employer.

22 21 20 19 18 17 16   10 9 8 7 6 5 4 3 2 1

Contents

ACKNOWLEDGMENTS

Erik Anderson for his patience in seeing this fun project through to the end; Sigrid Arnott for her tips on Native American fish signatures; Emmett Brown from the Freshwater Fishing Hall of Fame; Concordia University's Quasi Endowment Fund that helped pay the bills for this book; Chris Dorff for keeping lutefisk alive; Brad Hanson for his insights on herring production, even if it spills all over you; Geoff Johnson and his crazy fishing stories; Katy McCarthy for putting up with me on another one of these adventures; Heather Skinner for knowing how to get the word out like no one else; Peter Sorensen at the University of Minnesota for teaching me about the strange habits of fish and the stranger habits of humans; and Kristian Tvedten for his unbelievable ability to find great fishing images.

This classic photograph of two fishing friends with their catch of the day around 1900 required an artistic hand to level the fish and place the anglers in a perfect pose. COURTESY OF THE MINNESOTA HISTORICAL SOCIETY.

Fishing throughout Time

"THE GODS DO NOT SUBTRACT FROM THE ALLOTTED SPAN OF MEN'S LIVES the hours spent in fishing," advises an ancient Assyrian tablet from circa 2000 BCE. From the beginning, humans viewed fishing not only as an act of survival but also as a ritual of meditation. "God never did make a more calm, quiet, innocent recreation than angling," wrote Izaak Walton in *The Compleat Angler* from 1653. He described anglers as superior because of their contemplative pastime, as opposed to the blood sport of hunting. In fact, the phrase "gone fishin'" is synonymous with taking a break from the rat race.

This idea that fishing leads to tranquility and a loftier mentality is echoed throughout early texts. Washington Irving wrote, "There is certainly something in angling that tends to produce a serenity of the mind." President Herbert Hoover went further and declared, "All fishermen and fisherladies are by nature friendly and righteous persons. No one ever went to jail while fishing—unless they forgot to buy a license." Anglers, apparently, are somehow a notch above others.

This claim ignores the notorious exaggeration of catch size and yarns about dubious exploits. Perhaps the earliest such fish tale dates back to a smitten Mark Antony trying to impress his beloved Cleopatra. Most noble Romans did not fish for fun, but Cleopatra did on several occasions in the harbor of Alexandria with her royal entourage in tow. Plutarch, the Greek historian, wrote in AD 75 that Antony "went out one day to angle with Cleopatra, and, being so unfortunate as to catch nothing in the presence of

This marsh scene from the tomb of Menna predates Cleopatra by more than a millennium but shows the importance of fishing for the Egyptians. FACSIMILE (1924) OF ORIGINAL FROM CIRCA 1400–1352 BCE, METROPOLITAN MUSEUM OF ART.

his mistress, he gave secret orders to the fishermen to dive under water, and put fishes that had been already taken upon his hooks; and these he drew so fast that the Egyptian perceived it." Cleopatra feigned "great admiration" and invited her Roman suitor out to fish the next day. The following morning when Antony threw out his line, Cleopatra's servants secretly dove down and "fixed upon his hook a salted fish from Pontus. Antony, feeling his line give, drew up the prey, and, as may be imagined, great laughter ensued. 'Leave,' said Cleopatra, 'the fishing-rod, general, to us poor sovereigns of Pharos and Canopus; your game is cities, provinces, and kingdoms.'"

Fishing trickery is nothing new. "The one that got away" is inevitably triple the size of the little hammer handle that ends up in the frying pan. Hours spent trolling or holed up in an icehouse can only entice the imagination to create impossible stories to boast about this triumphant and daring sport. Illinois native Ernest Hemingway could have meant his novel *The Old Man and the Sea* to be about a lone

Opposite: President Herbert Hoover was an avid fisherman and often strolled into the water with a pipe and wearing a well-tailored suit. PHOTOGRAPH BY HARRIS & EWING, 1936. LIBRARY OF CONGRESS PRINTS AND PHOTOGRAPHS DIVISION.

A Day's Catch.

Greetings from *South Lake*, MICH.

Rarely did a fish weigh less than a fisherman in comical post-cards of the early twentieth century. COURTESY OF THE MINNE-SOTA HISTORICAL SOCIETY.

Midwestern fisherman; his sparse prose devoid of adjectives attempts to show the lack of hyperbole in the fantastic story. Building these incredible tales requires deadpan storytelling that sailors and fishermen have used for centuries. What is the trick to convince dubious onlookers? Always use fishing line that is far too weak for the task.

Despite these fish tales, fishing somehow kept its reputation as an enlightened sport. President Hoover wrote, "Fishing is much more than fish. It is the great occasion when we may return to the fine simplicity of our forefathers. . . . Next to prayer, fishing is the most

personal relationship of man." He went on to say that fishing is one of the times when you can tell others to shut up and revere this divine sport: "There are only two occasions when Americans respect privacy, especially in Presidents. Those are prayer and fishing."

Jesus himself used the sport as a metaphor in Matthew 4:19 when he told his disciples, "Follow me, and I will make you fishers of men." Fish became a symbol of Christianity, but evangelists took pains to

A ripping good fishing yarn could earn the teller membership in a "Liars Club." Clever tourism bureaus would tout the accuracy of fishing stories told in the lake country of northern Minnesota. *ABOVE:* COLLECTION OF DONALD HARRISON; *RIGHT:* SUMMERS PAST IN PARK RAPIDS.

clarify that the lost souls in this metaphor were to be swept up in nets rather than hooked (or tricked) by bait. Senior Pastor Wade Compton of Greenfield, Indiana, took this passage a bit more literally since he was tired of losing his congregation to the fishing boats on Sunday mornings. In 2013, he converted an old bait shop next to a lake as an annex for his United Methodist Church to attract "a new breed of worshipper." According to the Associated Press, August 16, 2013, Compton said, "They'll be at ease, and that's exactly where we want them to be . . . then after that, they get to go out and spend a couple of hours doing some free catch-and-release fishing in a stocked ten-acre lake that's loaded." Indeed, he's a fisher of fisher-

men. Writer Harmon Henkin in *Silent Seasons* took issue with the idea of fishing being somehow sacred: "Though some self-righteous evangelical preachers of the gospel of angling push the notion that the sport is conducted in a sublime and rarefied atmosphere, to me it has no greater claim to spiritual purity than sex, dope, or any other recreation in contemporary America."

Poet and preacher John Donne warned in 1619 that "the Devil angles with hooks and bayts; he deceives, and he wounds in the catching; for every sin hath his sting." An amazing exception is this medieval picture depicting God fishing for the Leviathan with Jesus as bait. FROM *HORTUS DELICIARUM (GARDEN OF DELIGHTS)*, COMPILED BY HERRAD OF LANDSBERG, 1185.

Though many civilizations claim to be first in fishing, the Chinese likely had the first reels, dating back to AD 300. Here is a detail from *Angler on a Wintry Lake*, the first known illustration of a fishing reel by the Chinese painter Ma Yuan in the thirteenth century.

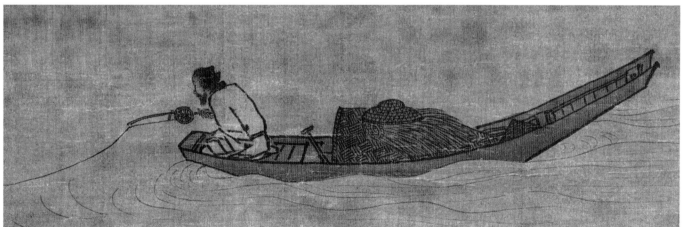

The first known reference to lutefisk in literature is from *History of the Nordic Peoples* from 1555 by Olaus Magnus. He wrote, "Soak dried fish two days in a strong lye solution and one day in fresh water to make fine food." *Fine* is the word that could be debated here.

Yet the stubborn tradition of fishing has a much stronger hold on our consciousness than some frivolous pastime. Angling likely extends as far back as hunting. Bone fishhooks discovered in the Czech Republic date back an astounding twenty thousand years. Other hooks unearthed in a cave in East Timor are from the Pleistocene epoch, around forty-two thousand years ago. Even the Bible links fishing to the earliest family and lays claim to the origin of this favorite pastime. Adam and Eve's son Seth "taught it to his sons, and that by them it was derived to posterity," according to *The Compleat Angler*.

Grandfathers passing their fishing prowess on to their kin can probably be traced back to antiquity,

just as the younger set protest these forced lessons to "build character." In *Leaving Home*, Garrison Keillor wrote, "Thank you, dear God, for this good life and forgive us if we do not love it enough. Thank you for the rain. And for the chance to wake up in three hours and go fishing: I thank you for that now, because I won't feel so thankful then." Minnesota musician John Perkins told me: "My uncle would drag me out of bed into the boat first thing in the morning. We'd jab hooks through these poor little minnows and throw the bleeding bait into the water or troll with a Bass Buster. I'd get a tug, so we would turn the boat around, but it was always just weeds. After hours of utter boredom in the scorching heat,

Joachim Beuckelaer's painting *Le Marché aux poissons* (The fish market) from 1568 captures the hustle and bustle of a commercial fish market in Renaissance Europe. MUSÉE DES BEAUX-ARTS DE STRASBOURG.

I'd have sun poisoning all across my body. Some fun! Uncle Bob mercifully let me off on shore. Then cousin Bob snagged his finger on a three-pronged hook with the other barb stuck in the wooden dock. He was attached to the dock and screaming his head off. Now he's the vice president of a bank."

Russian writer Sergei Aksakov takes issue with this type of characterization in *Notes on Fishing*: "The accusation of vacuity and idleness is entirely unjust. A true sportsman is necessarily bound to be very hale and very active: consider the early rising, often before dawn; enduring the damp and cold weather or the sultriness of midday . . . taken together this is not to the taste of a lazy man." In other words,

BROOK TROUT FISHING.

Fishing was not a time to be without a three-piece suit. In 1862, Currier & Ives printed *Brook Trout Fishing. "An Anxious Moment,"* showing a gentleman angler with his fresh catch on the rocky riverside. COURTESY OF THE MICHELE AND DONALD D'AMOUR MUSEUM OF FINE ARTS, SPRINGFIELD, MASSACHUSETTS. GIFT OF LENORE B. AND SIDNEY A. ALPERT, SUPPLEMENTED WITH MUSEUM ACQUISITION FUNDS. PHOTOGRAPHY BY DAVID STANSBURY.

fishing is the noble "strenuous life" that Teddy Roosevelt argued could build a better person.

Anglers are not only persistent and energetic but also creative. One of the oldest surviving texts on fishing, *Halieutica (Fishing),* written by Oppian of Cilicia in southern Turkey in the second century, details bizarre techniques from hooking eels with sheep intestines to cunning fishermen dressed as goats sneaking up on suspicious fish. Inexplicable fishing outfits are nothing new: the experimental nature of anglers to use their guiles and wiles to snag

an elusive fish forces them to accept disappointment and hope for the rare victory.

President Hoover again weighed in on the hardships: "There are two handicaps which apply to all expeditions for fish. The first is the depletion of your savings. You must buy more tackle; and you must bring one coat with large checks. . . . The second hardship relates to frustration. You have been dreaming for the previous six months about that big one. But your appointment with destiny will connect you with the smaller sizes." To fish is not to become rich, but one need not be rich to fish. Izaak Walton wrote three hundred years ago about the bitter ways of the wealthy who have no time to fish: "Men that are taken to be grave, because nature hath made them of a sour complexion; money-getting men, men that spend all their time, first in getting, and next in anxious care to keep it; men that are condemned to be rich, and then always busy or discontented; for these poor rich men, we Anglers pity them perfectly, and stand in no need to borrow their thought to think ourselves so happy."

Time is not money when fishing. The intangible reward for sitting in a lone boat on a cold lake is camaraderie. Anglers understand true friends can be comfortable together during those long silences. The three-time senator from Wyoming, Mike Enzi, recalled his meaningful fishing trips with Dick Cheney. The vice president, whose daughter was running against Enzi, had scrubbed this image from his memory when telling ABC's *This Week,* "Well, Mike also said he and I are fishing buddies, which is simply not true. Never happened." A shocked Enzi responded, "I thought we were friends." Considering

Brook trout fishing continued to be a popular pastime for men and women well into the twentieth century. COURTESY OF THE MINNESOTA HISTORICAL SOCIETY.

Cheney's track record of shooting a hunting buddy, Enzi should be thankful for the snub.

Obviously we find truth in the boat. We find out who our real pals are and how much we can endure of those biting blackflies nibbling on our ankles. We experience the essence of our history, of countless anglers before us over millennia trying to outwit the fish beneath the waves. We invent outrageous stories to tell those who slept in rather than risk the rain. And if we are lucky enough to reel in a walleye, we'll even have a delicious shore lunch. 🐟

Al's Bait & Tackle in Two Harbors, Minnesota, is an ideal place to stock up on fishing supplies before driving up the north shore of Lake Superior. PHOTOGRAPH BY THE AUTHOR.

CHAPTER ONE

The Right Stuff
Bait, Bobbers, and Knucklebusters

If people concentrated on the really important things in life, there'd be a shortage of fishing poles.

—*Wisconsin columnist Doug Larson*

The correct gear is essential for the fishing experience. Apart from the latest Lund boat, fillet knife, Shakespeare reel, and Mercury outboard, a true sign of dedication requires the funniest fishing hat and the most irreverent bumper sticker. T-shirts call out "Here fishy, fishy, fishy" in vain, and others cast little doubt on their Cartesian raison d'être with "I fish; therefore, I am." We only exist once we buy the fishing license at the beginning of the season and go to the lake.

From shiners to Rapalas to leeches, every self-respecting fisherman or fisherwoman has a secret lure or bait that fish can't resist. Unfortunately, the dumb fish don't know a good lure when they see one and sometimes prefer a beer pull tab to a ten-dollar Dardevle. Regardless, aficionados collect old lures and now demand top price for these relics to stuff their antique tackle boxes. Live bait doesn't keep,

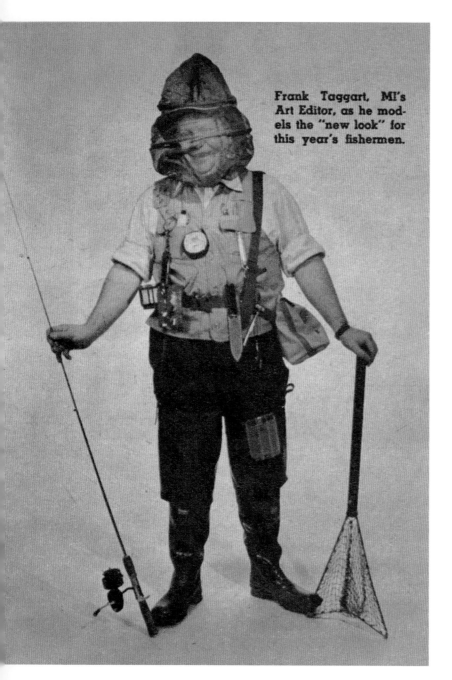

Frank Taggart, MI's Art Editor, as he models the "new look" for this year's fishermen.

Most modern anglers don't consider their clothes essential to snagging a good fish, but the earliest known fishing book, *Halieutica*, from the second century, recommends donning goat skins and horns to fool the fish. FROM ANDREA ALCIATO, *LES EMBLEMES*, PARIS, 1539. COURTESY OF GLASGOW UNIVERSITY LIBRARIES.

Mechanix Illustrated ran a spring feature, "New Gadgets for More Fish," that proclaimed that more than one million dollars are spent on new contraptions each year—and this was in May 1949! The magazine's art editor, Frank Taggart, tries on the latest garb.

but that doesn't stop designer bait shops from feeding leeches colorful food, turning these bloodsuckers bright neon shades to lure the big ones to the hook. Bait shops go beyond selling mere minnows and frequently double as the general store or offer unsavory combinations such as bakery and bait.

Dressed to Fish

From Oilskins to Goat Hides

The classic fishing outfit is a bucket hat, waders, and a tan vest with a dozen pockets. Now clothing manufacturers make specialty outfits—from hats to pants, from gaiters to gloves—to ensure maximum comfort for sport anglers.

Is this the best way to catch the big ones, though? The earliest known fishing book, *Halieutica*, by Oppian of Cilicia in the second century, describes how dressing up as a goat is the best way to fool fish. Perhaps this ploy could be employed by fly-fishing experts to sneak up to trick trout that are always wary of being snagged. Oppian describes a saltwater fish he called "Sargues," or sargo, that

> have their hearts possessed by affection for Goats. Goats they yearn for and they rejoice exceedingly in the mountain-dwelling beasts. . . . For when the goatherds bring their bleating flocks to the shore, to bathe in the eddying waves at noontide, at the

season when the hot Olympian star arises, then the Sargues, hearing the bleating on the shore and the deep murmur of the herds, rush all together in haste, sluggish though they be, and leap joyfully on the terraces by the sea and fawn upon the horned company and lick them. . . . [The wily fisherman then makes] his limbs clothed in the skin of a goat and two horns fastened to his temples . . . and he casts into the sea a bait of barley-meal enriched with goatflesh and roasted meat together. . . . Unhappy fishes! How fatal a friend they presently find him . . . for straightway he arrays against them a rough rod and a line of grey flax and puts on the hook the natural flesh of a goat's hoof. They greedily seize the bait and he with stout hand pulls and lands them.

Norwegian fishermen wore oiled wool sweaters to keep them toasty warm even when wet. CHRISTIAN EGGEN, *TWO MEN BY FISHING BOAT ON SHORE*, 1887. OIL ON CANVAS, 21½ × 28½ INCHES. 1991.063.002. GIFT OF BARBARA SOLBERG. COURTESY OF THE VESTERHEIM NORWEGIAN-AMERICAN MUSEUM, DECORAH, IOWA.

Early commercial fishermen always wore wool because it kept its warmth even when wet. Some fishing families, especially around the Great Lakes, even kept sheep for their fleece and knit sweater vests called "heart warmers." To prevent water from even getting to the wool, sailors and fishers covered up with oilskin: sailcloth made waterproof with tar or linseed oil sometimes coated with paint. Norwegian legends tell of Lofoten fishermen sleeping in their work clothes because they were so tired. The smell of fish permeated their wool sweaters, which were worn daily in the cold winter months. Fortunately for all those around, modern materials and washing machines keep fishers from smelling too fishy today.

Get the Gear

Hula Poppers, Tweetle Bugs, and Fuzzy Grubs

Muddler Minnow, Wooly Worm, Buzz Bullet, and Tinsel Tail are inventive names for modern lures that are guaranteed to put dinner on the table. But when did humans start using lures to trick fish? Fishhooks are among the earliest tools that archaeologists have uncovered. Digs in China and Egypt reveal bronze hooks and lines that date back to 2000 BCE. Homer describes in the *Odyssey* a cryptic fishing scene to trick the fish: "Casting into the deep the horn of an ox of the homestead, and as he catches each flings it up writhing, so writhing were they borne upward to the cliff." One reading of this is that Homer meant the horn as a hook or a lure, or perhaps it was bait, as Oppian of Cilicia described in his book how much fish liked goats.

Even though the Chinese used spun silk for lines centuries before anyone in the Mediterranean was fishing, Oppian is credited with the first description of fishing line in his treatise: "For straightway thou lettest from thy hand into the sea the well-woven line, and the fish quickly meets and seizes the hook of bronze and is speedily haled forth—not all unwilling—by our king; and thy heart is gladdened."

The Chinese likely used the first reels in the third century AD to wind up all that special silk. Modern reels date from the mid-1700s in Nottingham, England. This town is famous for Robin Hood but was also known for lace; a type of wooden bobbin was used to wind the line, and the reel was named after the town.

Beyond the basics of a rod, reel, and line, anglers have pondered for centuries about what will actually convince the fish to bite the hook. Tackle boxes full of classic and modern lures supposedly show how serious someone is about catching fish. The book *Fishing for Buffalo* warns, "The more fishing stuff you own, the ads tell us, the happier you'll be. But it doesn't work that way. Eventually more gear means more things to worry about, more repairs, more maintenance, and more things to lose." Even so, who can resist the prospect of the new gadget that will make everything easier?

While tackle stores are eager to promote the newest and best lures, fellow fishers are often wary about giving away their tricks. To throw off rival fishermen, *Field and Stream* writer John Merwin admitted, "I'll confess to a dirty trick. Before returning to a marina dock or my truck, I take the day's hot lures off my rods and put them away. To the same rods, I then attach lures that didn't work. That means the prying eyes of other anglers in the parking lot will be

The best part of fishing lures are the bizarre names that hook anglers with promises of catching the big one. From Dardevle to Lazy Ike, from Eureka Wiggler to Hula Popper, inventors had a semantic battle over the wildest nicknames. PHOTOGRAPHS BY THE AUTHOR.

The biggest one was that long-honestly. Get away? How could he—I used a VERNLEY ROD and a Y. & E Automatic Reel
And, by the way, how do you like my rain-proof Duxbak fishing suit? Pretty nice—what?

BEST — HORROCKS-IBBOTSON CO. UTICA. N.Y. MAKERS OF FISHING TACKLE. — BY TEST

Will you go fishing with me? Anyhow, drop me a line and I'll tell you how the fishing [UTICA] tackle, made by Horrocks-Ibbotson Co., will catch and hold the big ones. [UTICA] I know, and I'll tell you if you write me. Yours originally,

THE UTICA FISHING GIRL.

In 1917 the Horrocks-Ibbotson Company introduced anglers to the Utica Fishing Girl in a series of advertising postcards. "Will you go fishing with me?" she asks.

A well-stocked tackle box filled with scores of lures, lines, and reels is essential for any self-respecting angler. PHOTOGRAPH BY THE AUTHOR.

Tackle & tackle box
donated by Bob & Lois Helland
Lures donated by Al Baert,
Richard Jump, Loren Ortendahl,
Russel Atkinson & Paul Schmidt (see tags)

led astray." Is this dishonest, or is it just being protective of secrets?

Any tackle box will surely have a Rapala, a replica of a silvery minnow that floats on the water but dips down when the line is tugged. The trick is to twitch the line but not let it go down too far and snag weeds. Lauri Rapala founded the largest fishing lure manufacturer in the world in Finland in the 1930s, but it wasn't until 1959 that Ron Weber "discovered" this amazing lure and together with Ray Ostrom started Normark Corporation to market the lure stateside.

The best-known lure is probably the red-and-white-striped Dardevle spoon. Lou Eppinger from Detroit invented what he called the "Osprey" while on a fishing trip in Ontario in 1906. He renamed it after the Marines' Fourth Brigade "Devil Dogs" or "Teufelhunden," as the Germans called them, because of the fierce fighting during the Battle of Belleau Woods outside Paris in 1918. The new demonic name sparked protests when "some clergymen objected to 'devil,' hence the present 'Dardevle,'" according to Joe Fellegy's *Classic Minnesota Fishing Stories*.

The first commercially manufactured lure likely hails from Heddon and Pflueger of Michigan in the early nineteenth century. They made many different kinds of lures, but the Torpedo proved the most popular. Even though they are now considered classic, "these are lures that actually work," according to *Field and Stream*.

Another popular lure hailed from Fort Dodge, Iowa: the Lazy Ike. In *Classic Minnesota Fishing Stories*, Harry Van Doren wrote about a fisherman who introduced him to this strange lure in 1948. "The walleyes hit all of them. We trolled kind of fast, and when they hit the Lazy Ike they were hooked! Everybody went for Lazy Ikes after that day." At least until another lure, like the Jitterbug or Hula Popper, came along.

It's unusual for the president of the most powerful country in the world to endorse something as lowly as a lure, but Jimmy Carter proclaimed his preference for the Hawaiian Wiggler in his book *An Outdoor Journal*: "It seemed to go anywhere with-

out getting snagged; depending on the model, the arrangement of the skirt, and the speed of retrieval, the lure could be placed at almost any depth we desired. Bass were mesmerized by it." Carter made no comment on "The Prez" lure, which had eyes on a peanut-shaped lure made in honor of a fishing peanut farmer from Georgia who became the thirty-ninth president of the United States.

The Fish Are Biting!
The Only Limit Is the Size of the String

Fishermen riding colossal walleyes filled hand-colored postcards prior to the 1920s in the north woods. Trick photography, thanks to sleight of hand in the darkroom, made diminutive fishermen the bait for gigantic northern pike. Was this a ploy to keep strangers out of favorite fishing grounds or just another fish story? It's not known whether these joke postcards convinced gullible outsiders about the bounty in northern lakes, but actual snapshots show fishermen unable to even hold up their stringers of fish. Newspapers confirm the photographic record of these early fishing trips to the lakes that seemed too good to be true. The *Minnesota Democrat* wrote in August 1851, "Four gentlemen of St. Paul enjoyed a day sport at hunting and fishing last week, on Rice creek and Rice lake. They caught 300 pounds of black bass and killed 63 prairie chickens."

The *Weekly Minnesotian* confirmed this abundance of fish when Colonel John P. Owens wrote about a fishing trip in September 1852 to Lake Minnetonka. In need of lunch, a few "of the party cast in their lines, and quicker than it will take us to relate

Not only did trains allow hunters to fell buffalo from the comfort of the cars, but they opened up lakes to avid anglers. This elegant crowd, which includes Minnesota Governor John Lind (second man from right on the train), shows off their catch in 1899. COURTESY OF THE HENNEPIN COUNTY LIBRARY, MINNEAPOLIS PHOTO COLLECTION.

Longer strings make for better photographs! Around 1900, these four men show off their haul from Big Stone Lake in western Minnesota. COURTESY OF THE BIG STONE COUNTY HISTORICAL SOCIETY.

the fact, they flung to shore more bass than twelve hungry men could devour in one meal. They continued fishing fifteen or twenty minutes, and the product was about forty pounds—all bass of the largest size."

Trains that eventually connected this giant lake to the Twin Cities allowed a fisherman to haul back more than fifty fish from one day on the lake. "The length of the string was the limit. . . . The supply seemed inexhaustible," a fisherman reported at the time. Hotels on the lake would often clean the fish for patrons. Nellie Wright recounted to author Blanche Wilson about her family hosting fishermen at her hotel in the book *Minnetonka Story*: The guests "bring home so many fish, Ma and Pa would be up all night cleaning 'em. Next day we'd have fish every meal." At another hotel, according to Thelma Jones's *Once upon a Lake*, "So many fish were caught that the hotels did not always try to keep them separated. They were stored in sacks in the ice-houses and when there was no more room, the staff dug holes and quietly buried the fish."

Just as George Washington caught thousands of fish he couldn't possibly eat (and buried them for fertilizer), so did early fishermen in the Midwest. The *Hennepin County Mirror* complained about the wasted fish on Lake Minnetonka on April 8, 1880: The "long, cold winter is 'busted up' at last. Fish are running at 'good hickory' and 'tis very fortunate for some of the natives. We will have a square meal if the law don't interfere. . . . Tourists can catch them by the boat load, and cast them out on the banks to spoil."

President Herbert Hoover later complained of this excess when he wrote, "There is a particular belief that goes among most fishermen and that is that they have a divine right to unlimited fish." Supplies of fish in the north woods were thought to be inexhaustible, but many of the lakes suffered dramatic reductions in fish populations because of overfishing and netting. A limit was finally set in 1891 in Minnesota that only as many fish or animals could be caught as "can be used immediately for food purposes."

Peter Sorensen, fisheries professor at the University of Minnesota, asked me rhetorically, "Could we go back to those days with thousands of fish? Prob-ably so. The old stories are true about how many fish there were. They were giant and you could almost walk over the water on them. It was real and could happen again if we managed the lakes properly."

Taking the Bait

A Skinned Rabbit on a Hook

Classic bait shops carry on the long tradition of deciphering exactly what will catch a fish. Minnows, leeches, and night crawlers sometimes spend their last living moments on a hook to entice a walleye to chomp down, but centuries of trial and error have yielded surprises in the realm of bait. Some fishermen opt for bait "harnesses" that keep frogs and other little creatures alive longer as a more active attraction for the fish, or they prefer a small nylon bag to hold fish eggs that larger fish can't resist. *The Compleat Angler* from 1653 recommends a sympathetic treatment for the bait about to die: "I say, put your hook, I mean the arming wyer through his mouth, and out at his gills . . . and in so doing, use him as though you loved him, that is, harm him as little as you may possibly, that he may live the longer." Occasionally certain forms of bait are illegal (such as goldfish in Minnesota) or requirements call for killing bait, such as leeches, rather than setting them free in pristine lakes.

In European competitive fishing contests, anglers typically use "different types of maggots, called 'pinkies,' 'gozzers,' 'squats,' and 'jokers.' These are bred on decaying pigeons or chickens and are often dyed orange, bronze or blue," according to *Fishing for*

Grasshoppers once swarmed fertile fields and devastated crops. Who would have thought that destitute farmers could turn these hoppers into cash by selling them as bait? PHOTOGRAPH BY THE AUTHOR.

Buffalo. Certain fish love this foul bait. Minnesota fisherman Geoff Johnson says he'll try anything smelly: "I use rotten chicken livers to catch catfish." This idea of feeding one creature to another because they will eat any old thing was echoed by Mark Twain when Huckleberry Finn remembers, "The first thing we done was to bait one of the big hooks with a skinned rabbit and set it and catch a cat-fish that was as big as a man, being six foot two inches long, and weighed over two hundred pounds. . . . We found a brass button in his stomach and a round ball, and lots of rubbage." Was this based on Twain's own experience growing up in Hannibal, Missouri, along the Mississippi River?

Smell is key, so anglers experiment with Lunker Lotion, Worm Oil, and Dr. Juice Steelhead Elixir as the snake oils that may catch the prize fish. Dick Sternberg in *The Art of Freshwater Fishing* says, "Oils and gels appeal to the fish's sense of smell. They are applied to plastic worms, plugs, and live bait. Catfish anglers use stinkbaits, cheese, and dried blood." President Herbert Hoover recommended something far simpler: "All American small boys spit on the bait." Hank Kehborn confirmed youngsters' fortune in *Classic Minnesota Fishing Stories* when he described trying different lures and bait and then came home without any fish—only to find his wife cooking up great bass fillets that his children had caught. "And you know what they were using for bait? They caught that beautiful stringer of largemouth bass on bubblegum, pink bubblegum!"

"Grocery bait" consists of anything from marshmallows to stinky cheese to canned corn, apparently a favorite of catfish. The Freshwater Fishing Hall of Fame in Hayward, Wisconsin, features a tackle box from an Arkansas catfisherman that had large compartments for liver, dough balls, and other fragrant treats. All anglers in search of flathead catfish have their own bizarre recipes for dough balls. *Fishing for Buffalo* recommends ingredients such as "vanilla, anise, molasses, beer, whiskey, bourbon, strawberry Jell-O, cornmeal, grated cheese, cinnamon, cocoa, honey, onion, garlic, wheat germ, cottonseed oil, corn germ, cereal, eggs, crackers . . ." This seems like health food compared to the putrid rotting maggots that European anglers sometimes use.

Perhaps the technique comes from the earliest surviving book on fishing, *Halieutica (Fishing)* from the second century. The author, Oppian of Cilicia, shows a clever fisherman using sheep intestines to catch the elusive eel. "He takes a long sheep-gut and

— LUMINOUS BAIT —

1ST FISHER.
HELLO BURK! HOW DID YOU CAPTURE THAT FINE STRING OF FISH? I'VE BEEN OUT SINCE MORNING AND HAVE ONLY A FEW MEASLY PERCH.
2D FISHER.
OH! THIS IS ONLY THREE HOURS WORK! MY TIME IS TOO VALUABLE DURING THE DAY. SO I GO EVENINGS I USE **PFLUEGER'S LUMINOUS BAIT.**
3D FISHER.
HA! I'VE HEARD THAT THE GAME FISH REST DURING THE DAY AND FEED AT DARK. I'LL USE THE **LUMINOUS BAIT** HEREAFTER.

Luminous bait, now common among fishing equipment, appeared in tackle boxes as early as the 1890s. This promotional illustration is from the Detroit and Cleveland Steam Navigation Company's publication *A Lake Tour to Picturesque Mackinac via the D. & C.* (Detroit: O. S. Gilley, Bornman and Company, 1890).

lets it trail its length in the water, like a long line. The Eel espies it and rushes up and seizes it. The youth perceives that the Eel has swallowed the bait and straightway blows in the sheep gut and inflates it with his breath. By his vehement blowing the gut swells up and fills the straining mouth of the wretched Eel; which is straitened and distressed by the human breath, but is held a fast prisoner for all its endeavor to escape, until, swollen and wildly gasping, it swims to the surface and becomes the prey of the fisher." The intestine is still inside the eel and contributes a special flavor when these snake-like fish are roasted.

Breeding Leeches
Squiggling "Black Gold"

According to the Congressional Sportsmen's Foundation, 1.1 billion dollars are spent annually in the United States on bait. No wonder Phil DeVore of Superior, Wisconsin, became a "leech wrangler," or a "leech entrepreneur," as he calls himself.

A simple leech trap consists of a metal coffee can pinched nearly closed at the top. Slip in samples of stinky chicken livers and submerge the can in mucky water. Lift the can before sunrise to trap the nocturnal *Nephelopsis obscura*, ribbon leeches, which have slithered through the opening at night. These are the best leeches for bait and won't suck your blood if they get hungry.

With a master's degree in fisheries from Michigan State University, DeVore used his knowledge of life below the waves to start a leech "ranch." He buys little bloodsuckers in the spring and places them in ponds on his land. He expanded the idea of simple leech traps a step further and began what he calls a "feed-lot operation" of "black gold." Careful not to tumble into the drink himself, DeVore paddles a canoe on his pond to feed the leeches "ground-up fish organs, beef and turkey liver, whatever meat he can find that someone wants to get rid of," wrote Sam Cook in the *Duluth News Tribune*.

By 2001, DeVore had raised several million leeches, approximately twelve thousand pounds, according to the *News Tribune*. He checks on his slithery creatures daily during the summer to ensure they are fattening up nicely to make a good dinner for a fish. "People always ask me, 'Do you ever eat 'em?' I can't afford to. Steak is much cheaper." Besides, he has all the bait he needs to catch his fill.

Beer companies like Minneapolis's own Grain Belt recognized that anglers represented a perfect market for their suds. What better way to tempt a thirsty fisher than giving away free beer bobbers?

Look for the Light

Bobbing for Beer and Mermaids

Early anglers used cork or balsa wood for bobbers to suspend the hooked bait at a desired depth in the water for fish to strike. Heavier bait required more buoyant bobbers, and light bait used sensitive, thin ones that wiggled when a little fish nibbled. Plastic allowed for all sorts of modifications. Beer companies branded bobbers with their logos and gave them away so that fishermen watching the floating plastic Grain Belt Beer diamond would remember it was time to crack open another can.

Air Light of Omaha envisioned sirens of the sea luring fishermen into the waves, so its Mermaid Bobber hit the shelves available as a hand-painted blonde, brunette, or redhead. Two companies in South Bend, Indiana, had the same idea. The most popular, the Virgin Mermaid from Stream-Eze, "lures both men and fish. In your Tackle Box, she's a 'DOLL'—in the water she is a 'wow' with action and alure," according to its packaging. Tempting the public with mermaids was made famous by the great nineteenth-century purveyor of trickery P. T. Barnum. He began his career as a patent medicine salesman and got rich selling fantasies and humbugs to people, most of whom, he found, "appear disposed to be amused even when they are conscious of being deceived." In 1842, he plastered New York City with posters promoting the beautiful mermaid on display

This 1959 advertisement (the second in a three-part series) for Western Fishing Line told the tale of Gus the fisherman, who accidentally snagged a gorgeous mermaid. "G'wan, scram!" he yelled. "Can't a guy fish in peace without some dizzy fish-tail dame butting in?" The feisty siren replied, "I can't, stupid. I'm hooked right in the—well, see for yourself." Embarrassed, Gus helped her unhook herself but was far more interested in fishing.

SNOOPY takes a nap, gently floating in the water until fish bite. Then he pops up in a flash to let Little Anglers know there's a fish nibbling. A perfect match for Zebco youth tackle "Catch 'em" kits.

FROM ZEBCO

WOODSTOCK: © 1965 United Feature Syndicate, Inc.

Even Peanuts creator Charles Schulz got in on the fishing tackle game when the Snoopy Catch 'Em Bobber was introduced in the mid-1960s.

a flash to let Little Anglers know there's a fish nibbling." If that weren't enough to tell you when a sunfish has taken the bait, special bobbers trigger a switch to illuminate a bulb in a plastic shell when the fish bite.

Bobbers soon became a symbol of fishing, so the town of Pequot Lakes in north central Minnesota sloshed dozens of gallons of red and white paint on its water tower to make Paul Bunyan's bobber. A tall tale arose that the giant lumberjack was fishing with his new bobber made by his Swedish blacksmith Ole. Paul snagged Notorious Nate the Northern from the lake and heaved him from the water with his giant fishing pole. The crater Nate made when he dropped from the sky is where pots of beans are slow-cooked overnight for the annual Bean Hole Days in Pequot Lakes, and the sixty-foot bobber conveniently ended up on giant stilts to provide the town's drinking water.

A retelling of an Ojibwe legend states that Nanabojo, the trickster, challenged mighty Paul Bunyan to a duel after the Native American hero had seen the lumberjack greedily strip the forests of trees. The battle lasted for weeks, and the northland shook with the wrestling match, just as it had when Paul wrestled with Babe the Blue Ox. The Ojibwe version says that Nanabojo beat poor ol' Paul silly with a giant fish.

at his museum. When the masses paid twenty-five cents admission, they encountered a fish tail sewn to the body of a dried monkey. The people kept coming, content in their newfound knowledge that advertisements were goofy exaggerations—good for a laugh but not to be taken too seriously.

To attract kids to fishing, Charles Schulz allowed his famous beagle to snooze on the waves. The Snoopy Catch 'Em Bobber "takes a nap, gently floating in the water until fish bite. Then he pops up in

The "Coffee Grinder"

Evinrude's Engine to Fetch Ice Cream for His Beloved

Ole Evinrude may have been a master tinkerer, but he was not so good at bookkeeping or balancing a budget. Fortunately, his peach of a neighbor, Bess Cary, had a knack for numbers and could handle the figures while Ole invented in his workshop. To impress his accountant (and now fiancée), Evinrude took her to the creamery for newfangled iced treats, but the five-mile trip in an open rowboat with temperatures rising to a scorching 90 degrees did not impress his betrothed. As soon as he returned home, he envisioned creating an alternative power source for his boat so his girlfriend's ice cream wouldn't melt. An early Evinrude advertisement from 1909 declared, "Don't row! Throw the oars away! Use an Evinrude motor!"

Thomas Reccc of Philadelphia had already invented the first "portable" marine propeller, or outboard motor, in 1866. The problem was that the giant hunk of metal could not be easily moved, so it wasn't much better than expensive and ubiquitous inboard engines. Evinrude made his first outboard motor in 1907, which his new wife Bess called the "coffee grinder." Others called these early engines "knucklebusters" because operators had to let go in a hurry after yanking the line to rev the little engine to life. To go backward, the rope needed to be wound in the opposite direction on top of the motor. Evinrude made a better-looking motor in 1909 and lent it to a friend for a test drive. His buddy placed orders for ten motors, and within four years Evinrude outboards were for sale around the world.

Evinrude Outboard Motors of Milwaukee declared a challenge in 1913 that this young woman could overtake any boat propelled by a rival Johnson motor. PHOTOGRAPH BY R. R. JOHNSTONE. LIBRARY OF CONGRESS PRINTS AND PHOTOGRAPHS DIVISION.

Evinrude was not without competition. Submerged Electric Motor Company of Menominee, Wisconsin, built an outboard to run on batteries—which were too pricy, and the company went belly up in 1909. Thirty-eight more outboard motor companies sprang up in the Upper Midwest, and with them new innovations. Finally, in 1915, Adolph and Arthur Caille of Detroit invented a self-winding starter that made the tedious "knucklebusters" passé.

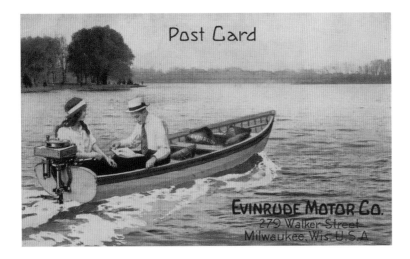

In Terre Haute, Indiana, three Johnson brothers assembled a one-cylinder inboard engine in the blacksmith shop of their father. Louis, Clarence, and Harry Johnson were so pleased with the result that they established the Johnson Motor Company in 1921. The following year, the brothers completed the first lightweight outboard motor. This Light Twin, with two horsepower and made almost completely out of aluminum, could easily be carried since it weighed only thirty-five pounds and was affordable at $135. The company set a speed record for outboard engines in 1926 with its Big Twin at 16 miles per hour. Johnson advertisements boasted "the snappiest motor that ever pushed a boat—and by far the easiest to carry."

Sixty-seven outboard motor companies started up in the early 1900s, but the Great Depression sunk most of them. Of the outboard manufacturers in the area, only Johnson, Mercury, and Evinrude survived into modern times and contributed to the more than ten million of these motors registered in 2015 in the United States alone. Because of this flurry of invention by Johnson, Evinrude, and others in the Upper Midwest, the Manitowoc Maritime Museum of Wisconsin declared the area the "outboard capital of the world."

Evinrude's affordable "Light Twin" revolutionized the outboard engine. Its aluminum construction made it truly portable; it weighed thirty-five pounds and could provide two horsepower. COURTESY OF THE MINNESOTA HISTORICAL SOCIETY.

YOUR GUIDE TO OUTBOARD MOTORING'S BIG BUYS

● Here are America's *quality* outboard motors. These are the outboards that are noted for DEPENDability! Here is the right power for every outboard need — from canoe to cruiser. See your Johnson Dealer. Look for his name under "Outboard Motors" in your classified phone book.

1 SEA-HORSE 25. New sensation of the waterways! 25 hp, 98 lbs. Speeds over 30 mph. *Yet it trolls!* Gear Shift. Twist-Grip Speed Control. Mile-Master. Everything deluxe! *And only* **$390.00***

2 SEA-HORSE 10. Finest fishin' motor a man can carry! 10 hp. *Smooth,* from heady speed to steady troll! Gear Shift. Twist-Grip. Mile-Master. Completely modern. And now priced at only **$275.00***

3 MILE-MASTER. Standard equipment with Sea-Horses 10 and 25. Modern fuel supply system (6 gal.) that extends your cruising range. Positive automatic pressure feed with plug-in, *self-sealing* connector. Leak-proof.

4 SEA-HORSE 5. America's largest-selling outboard! The happy combination of power, weight, features. One-pull starting. Neutral Clutch. Synchro-Control. *No shear pin.* Mr. DEPENDable himself! **$187.50***

5 SEA-HORSE 3. The rugged little twin with the big 3 hp push. Only 32 lbs! With Johnson's amazing weed-free, shoal-riding Angle-matic Drive **$145.00***

6 SHIP-MASTER REMOTE CONTROL. Shift-and-throttle operation at your steering wheel! *Corrosion proof.* Fits special built-in snap connectors on Sea-Horses 10 and 25. *Instant* hook-up **$29.50***

FREE! Write for the new Sea-Horse Catalog that describes the 4 great Johnsons for 1953 — all Perfected Alternate Firing Twins. Complete specifications.

JOHNSON MOTORS, 100 Pershing Road, Waukegan, Illinois
In Canada: Manufactured by Johnson Motors, Peterborough

 Prices f.o.b. factory, subject to change. Weights approx. OBC Certified brake hp at 4000 rpm.

THE ONLY MANUFACTURER WHO HAS BUILT A MILLION OUTBOARD MOTORS

Johnson SEA-HORSES
for DEPENDability

Suddenly, catching fish required a Sea-Horse. Johnson's outboard engine could be carried easily, unlike those stringers of giant fish. This advertisement from 1953 features six of Johnson's best products.

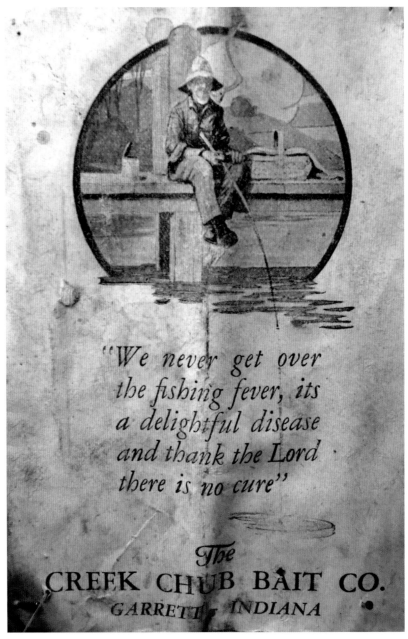

"We never get over the fishing fever, its a delightful disease and thank the Lord there is no cure"

The CREEK CHUB BAIT CO. GARRETT, INDIANA

Whimsical fishermen's sayings were often used in advertising, like this one for the Creek Chub Bait Company. PHOTOGRAPH BY THE AUTHOR.

Fear No Fish!

Slogans and Bumper Stickers

Fishing has been appropriated as a metaphor that anyone can understand. "Fish or cut bait" means you either stay in the game or leave. "Not his kettle of fish" is synonymous with "not his cup of tea." "Hook, line, and sinker" expresses the naïveté of someone who believed a lie, just as the Norwegian expression "take everything for good fish" refers to a gullible fool who assumes any fish, or deal, is worthwhile.

The art of telling a good story is essential to fishing, and making clever quips is highly regarded to break up all the quiet time in the boat. T-shirt slogans often spoof famous sayings:

- Bible: Give a man a fish, feed him for a day. Teach a man to fish, and he will sit in a boat and drink beer all day.
- Benjamin Franklin: Early to bed, early to rise, fish all day, make up lies.
- William Shakespeare: To fish or not to fish . . . Not to fish? As if that's even an option.
- Harley-Davidson: Live to fish; fish to live.

If a famous philosopher or writer can't be parodied, a new one-liner is born, as long as it fits on a bumper sticker:

- It's called "fishing" not "catching."
- Carpe ~~diem~~ carpium! (Seize the ~~day~~ carp!)
- A bad day of fishing is still better than a good day at the office.
- Fisherman: a jerk on one end of the line waiting for a jerk on the other.
- Born to fish. Forced to work.

- When in doubt, exaggerate.
- A woman who has never seen her husband fishing doesn't know what a patient man she married.
- Fishing isn't a matter of life and death. It's much more important.
- If guns don't kill people, but people kill people, does that mean that fishermen don't fish fish, fish fish fish?
- A, B, C, D, Eat Fish
- If wishes were fishes, we'd have a fish fry.
- Old fishermen never die; they just smell like they did.
- There's a fine line between fishing and standing on the shore like an idiot.
- Women want me; fish fear me.
- A fish wouldn't get caught if it kept its darn mouth shut.
- I support catch and eat.
- Fish tremble at the sound of my name.
- Good things come to those who bait.
- Sorry I'm late, but fishing takes so much time. 🐟

THE KIND WE CATCH HERE.

GREETINGS FROM ONAMIA, MINN.

HERE'S THE FISH I PROMISED YOU.

GREETINGS FROM AITKIN, MINN.

The summertime hijinks of intrepid fishermen were depicted on countless postcards advertising the angling hot spots of the north woods. AUTHOR'S COLLECTION.

CHAPTER TWO

The Wonderful, Weird World of Fishing

Pranksters, Monsters, and Female Fish Impersonators

A bad day of fishing always beats a good day of work.

—*Midwestern proverb*

Fish behavior is far stranger than we ever knew, and ichthyologists are just starting to unravel some of their secrets. Who would have believed that fish mating rituals to find true love beneath the waves involve female impersonators and fake orgasms?

Perhaps even more bizarre is human behavior above the surface. How can one explain why the U.S. Commission of Fish and Fisheries would haul in "carp by the carload" to stock our lakes with these invasive species for the rest of time? Many of the most foolish acts are done in the light of day and on a large scale. Fortunately, anglers are always up for a challenge, especially when these carp are then declared "the world's greatest sportfish," whether true or not.

We have imagined all the terrible prehistoric sea serpents in the deep waiting to gobble us up, whereas in reality the fish are in far more danger from us—unless the conservation officer nabs poachers with multiple lines in the water or engaged in other illegal activities. Fishing criminals are usually not so clever, and even a ditty sung by Big Mouth Billy Bass is enough to scare off skittish thieves.

Fake Muskies and Other Tricks

Daniel Boone Covered in Fish Guts

Typically, fishing writers tend to wax poetic about how sublime the sport is. Izaak Walton declared in *The Compleat Angler* in 1653, "Angling is somewhat like Poetry. . . . He that hopes to be a good angler must not only bring an inquiring, searching, observing wit, but he must bring a large measure of hope and patience, and a love and propensity to the Art itself." Walton didn't mention, however, a sense of fun and trickery.

Even frontiersman Daniel Boone showed an amazing lack of humor when he was a youthful lad asleep on the banks of the Schuylkill River. While the rugged young outdoorsman dozed, his mother, Sarah Morgan, caught fish and cleaned them on the bank. A couple of neighbor girls snuck up on Daniel and dumped the bucket of fish guts over the sleeping boy. Covered in slime, he jumped up and thrashed the girls, who ran home with bloody noses. The girls' mother returned to demand an explanation from the unchivalrous Daniel Boone who had hit young ladies. "They are not girls," he replied indignantly, according to Boone's biographer John Mack Faragher. "Girls would not have done such a dirty trick. They are row-

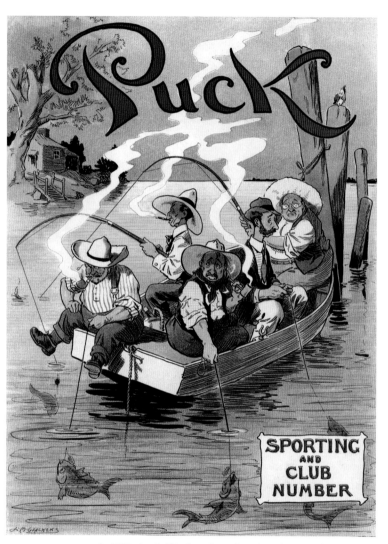

In 1910, Louis Glackens introduced readers to a dopey group of anglers, "The Tightwad Fishing Club," on the cover of *Puck* magazine. Each of the fishermen refuses to complete their catch by pulling the fish into the boat because the first to do so must treat the others. LIBRARY OF CONGRESS PRINTS AND PHOTOGRAPHS DIVISION.

In this staged photograph, Eugene Shepard and friends capture a "mythical beast," the hodag, which smelled like a mix between a buzzard and a skunk and had the head of a bull with a demonic grin. COURTESY OF THE WISCONSIN HISTORICAL SOCIETY, WHI-36382.

dies." His mother apparently believed him and told the girls' mother, "If thee has not brought up thy daughters to better behavior, it was high time they were taught good manners. They got no more than they deserved."

Anglers must always be ready for a trick to be

played on them. Fisherman Jake Cline from Hackensack, Minnesota, in *Classic Minnesota Fishing Stories*, recalls a friend who used to keep multiple lines in the holes of his icehouse. Cline put an old car spring down into the hole. "I took one of his tip-up lines, a heavy line, and tied it to the car spring. Then I let it down into his fish hole. Well, the guy saw that his line was down. He ran out there and started pullin'." He couldn't reel it in, and the line broke. Another friend teased him, "I thought you knew how to fish! Lose a big fish like that!" The foiled fisherman kept telling everyone about the giant fish he lost, until Cline told him about the trick the following year. He was not pleased.

Perhaps the best prankster of all was Eugene Shepard of Rhinelander, Wisconsin. Locals called him the "P. T. Barnum of Northern Wisconsin" since he always had some questionable scheme to make a buck or trick greenhorns. Shepard doctored photographs for newspapers around the country to publicize his "discovery" of a new monstrous species, the "bovine spirituallis" or hodag (horse-dog), which smelled like a buzzard but looked like a devilish ox with a spiked tail.

Shepard started a fishing resort in northern Wisconsin around 1900. He declared Ballard Lake the "Greatest Muskellunge Fishing of the World," but bored visitors went for hours in the boat without a

bite. He rigged up an elaborate system of wires that triggered springs under the water so fake muskies would jump out of the water just far enough away

Dame Juliana Berners allegedly wrote the first book in English on fishing. The "fishing nun" (whose existence has been doubted) published her *Treatisse on Fysshynge* in the late 1400s. COURTESY OF HEIDELBERG UNIVERSITY LIBRARY, *CODEX MANESSE*, PAGE 302R.

that no one could tell that they were not real. The anglers figured they were not using the right bait to catch the big ones, but they were certainly there under the waves. Reservations boomed, and he kept his prank secret.

Colonial Fishing

Cod Tongues and Fish Bladders

British colonists in America brought with them a love of fishing. Although fishing was largely left to the men, the first book in English on the sport was likely written by Dame Juliana Berners, a nun who lived near St. Albans, England, and loved the sport. Her *Treatyse on Fysshynge with an Angle* was published in 1496 and raised eyebrows when it equated fly-fishing with the more regal pastimes of hunting.

Briton Izaak Walton expanded on this text in *The Compleat Angler* and formatted the book as a discussion between a Piscator (fisherman), a hunter, and a falconer about the merits of fishing. This dialogue was a common format to address readers' questions. Even Galileo used this setup in 1632 to present the theory that the earth revolves around the sun and deflect any criticism that he himself was advocating this idea. Despite his obvious affinity for fishing, Walton took this tack to avoid diminishing hunt-

WIRING PIKE.

One seemingly impossible trick for catching lazy pickerel is "wiring" or "snaring" the oblivious fish as shown in this illustration from an 1824 edition of *The Compleat Angler, or The Contemplative Man's Recreation* by Izaak Walton and Charles Cotton.

27

ing and falconry and the royal preference for these sports.

Fishing in the New World proved far superior to fishing in England because the fish were "lying so thick with their heads aboue the water," according to Captain John Smith at Jamestown. He was describing the waters of the Potomac that bubbled with fish. Lacking a net, the group tried to catch them in frying pans, which proved useless. Instead, Smith wrote, "I amused myself by nailing them to the ground with my sword."

Soon enough, regular harvests of fish supplemented the colonists' diets. With the netting, however, came conflicts. When Daniel Boone was a boy, his family declared war on the fishermen downstream from them on the Schuylkill River who illegally dammed the river to catch shad so the fish could not travel upstream in the spring. The Boones staged a sneak attack on April 20, 1738, by canoeing into the area with clubs to break up the wooden dams. One of the defenders, John Wainwright, was left "as Dead with his Body on the Shoar & his ffeet in the River," according to records from the time. The attackers didn't succeed in enforcing the law and were fought off.

George Washington wasn't above the fracas either. This story, told by Washington Irving in *Life of George Washington* in 1856, stands as a likely apocryphal fish tale alongside the yarn of young George chopping down cherry trees and refusing to tell a lie. George Washington protected his fishing waters off Mount Vernon. One day he heard a trespasser shoot a rifle from a canoe. The indignant Washington rode to the river, where he met the culprit, who "raised his

Presidential politics requires the election of good fishermen. Pictured here is George Washington's original fishing tackle.
PHOTOGRAPH BY J. A. ANDERSON, 1906. LIBRARY OF CONGRESS PRINTS AND PHOTOGRAPHS DIVISION.

gun with a menacing look; but Washington rode into the stream, seized the painter of the canoe, drew it to shore, sprang from his horse, wrested the gun from the hands of the astonished delinquent, and inflicted on him a lesson in 'Lynch law' that effectually cured him of all inclination to trespass again on these forbidden shores."

Washington caught fish to sell in Alexandria and ship as far away as Antigua. (He later took advantage of his executive power to sign a law making whiskey production more lucrative and started his own alcohol business at Mount Vernon.) Washington wrote in his diary that his load of fish was "abt. 300 in one Hawl." In the year 1771, he snagged 79,000 herring and 7,760 shad from the Potomac, which was far more than he could sell or eat, so he used much of the catch simply as fertilizer on his land. He stored a lot of the fish to keep "a sufficiency of fish for the use of my own people."

The third U.S. president, Thomas Jefferson, was born in the town of Shadwell, Virginia, in 1743 and grew up netting shad in the Rivanna River. Although colonial scholars claim that Jefferson adored "shad-roe soufflé," writer John McPhee uncovered that Jefferson "liked his fresh shad laid open, broiled, and addressed with pepper, salt, and butter." He enjoyed other unusual fish parts as well, such as their "sounds," or air bladders. He wrote about his search for such delicacies in his July 1809 diary when he placed an order for "Cod's tongues and sounds. 1 keg."

Before Jefferson was born, the first angling club in the United States was founded in 1732 in Andalusia, Pennsylvania. The Schuylkill Fishing Company claims to be the longest continuously running club in the English-speaking world and the "oldest dining club in the world," according to the *New York Times*. George Washington and General Lafayette were honorary members. One tradition is to raise a glass of fish house punch to George Washington, who was known to put away a bottle of Madeira wine at every lunch. Another unusual ritual that was followed for a while had members wearing Mandarin hats in acknowledgment of all the American ginseng being sent to China. In the 1830s, the club hired an official worm digger.

According to John McPhee in *The Founding Fish*: "In 1832, on its hundredth anniversary, a hundred people (members and guests) sat down to a dinner that featured eleven pounds of food for each eater, and included, overall, forty-nine pounds of shad." The menu included 107 pounds of "beef, four pigs, thirty pounds of tongue, forty pounds of oysters, and twelve lobsters averaging 3.3 pounds." To wash it all down, the guests guzzled an average of thirty-four ounces of alcoholic beverages each, including eleven gallons of fortified wine and seventeen gallons of rum and brandy to strengthen their famous fish house punch. Even though Dame Juliana Berners wrote the first treatise in English on fishing, she wouldn't have been able to attend this fantastic luncheon at the Schuylkill Fishing Company because of its men-only policy.

Fish as Signatures

Totems and Effigy Mounds

In 1820, John C. Calhoun, Secretary of War, sent Lewis Cass to survey western Michigan Territory, of which Cass was governor. A group of forty-two men in voyageur canoes set out from Detroit to Wisconsin, Minnesota, Iowa, and the eastern Dakotas, which all were part of Michigan at the time. Henry Schoolcraft traveled with the expedition and later wrote one of the definitive guides to the territory. The twenty-one-year-old secretary of the trip, James Doty, kept a diary to record the findings of this diverse group that included Canadian voyageurs and Native Americans, mostly Ojibwe who had been loyal to the British (and some resented the American expedition). Toward the end of his journal, Doty asked the Native Americans to record their names in his book. Five were named for fish: "A-was-se-se," or small catfish; two were "Kenon-jai," or pike; and another two were "Tickiming," or white fish. Each drew the corresponding fish in his diary, essentially as a signature.

An earlier explorer through the area had already

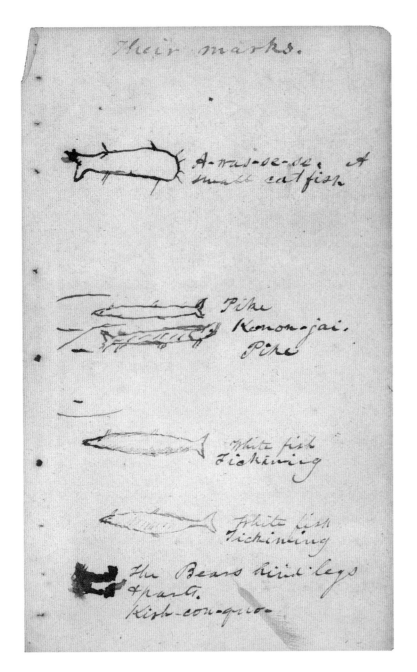

found Native American rock carvings of fish and other animals. Perhaps these were a sort of early signature graffiti. Jonathan Carver was sent by the British king to explore this uncharted area in 1766. He described in his journal discovering an enormous cave, in what is now St. Paul, filled with "many Indian hieroglyphicks, which appeared very ancient," of fish and animals. The native Dakota called it "Wakon-teebe," or "The House of the Great Spirit," and probably knew about the sacred cave for centuries.

"Carver's Cave" remained a must-see tourist attraction for European settlers to Minnesota. A letter in the *Minnesota Pioneer* from December 12, 1849, raves about the site:

> The cave is so large, you can walk erect in it for thirty or forty yards, when suddenly you find yourself in a room more beautiful than could be made with all the wealth of Astor. It is circular, about 15 feet in diameter, and high enough for the greatest beauty. Its floor, and walls, and siding, are all formed of this almost snow-white rock. In its centre is a large vase, smooth and white, and polished as marble, three or four feet in diameter, and about a foot in depth. . . . After you leave this room by creeping some distance, you find yourself in another room. . . . It gives rise to strange feelings to be in that narrow, winding passage, three hundred yards under ground.

When Henry Schoolcraft ventured west in 1820, he brought with him a secretary, James Duane Doty, who recorded the names and signature marks of their Native American guides in the expedition's official journal. COURTESY OF THE WISCONSIN HISTORICAL SOCIETY.

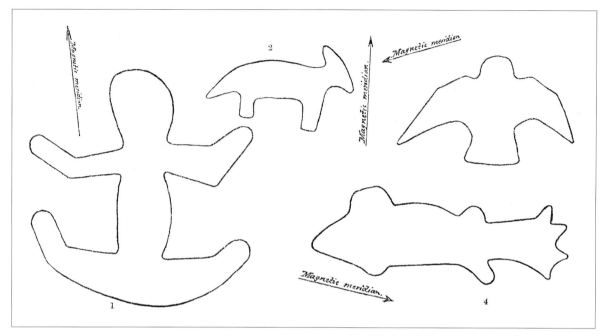

An outline of a fish-shaped effigy mound *(lower right)* measuring 110 feet was found near the Mississippi River at Winona, Minnesota. Unfortunately, eager farmers plowed over the sacred site. FROM T. H. LEWIS, "NOTICE OF SOME RECENTLY DISCOVERED EFFIGY MOUNDS," *SCIENCE* 5, NO. 106 (FEBRUARY 13, 1885): 131–32.

In 1879, the carvings were still visible; a tour guide remarked about the etchings of "snakes, birds, men, animals, fish, and turtles." The City of St. Paul let railroad construction cut away about half of the House of the Great Spirit even though the cave had been regarded as "the foremost relic of antiquity" in the state. Today, a fence guards the opening of what is left of the sacred site.

Just as petroglyphs of fish disappeared, so did many of the Indian mounds. The burial mounds were along prominent spots on rivers and lakes. The largest in the upper Midwest are the Grand Mounds near the Canadian border at International Falls, Minnesota. Archaeologists hypothesize that these forty-foot-high mounds, which measured 325 feet in circumference, were built by the ancient Laurel Indians who were lured to the area by the giant sturgeon filling the lakes. An unusual effigy mound in the shape of a fish near Winona was discovered in 1884. The Dakota Group of mounds, only thirty feet from the Mississippi River in Winona, stood about three feet tall and 110 feet long. Surveyor T. H. Lewis wrote about his findings: "The tail is four-lobed and on the body are three projections, suggesting that the mound is an effigy of a fish with fins." The fish effigy mound has been plowed over, so little remains of these early Native American images of fish.

A Carload of Fish.

Trick photography usually boasted of fishermen hauling in a lunker bigger than their boat, but here the fish barely fits on a flatbed! The irony is that the U.S. Commission of Fish and Fisheries sent carloads of carp by train to breed in lakes and rivers around the country. Oops! POSTCARD BY J. HERMAN, 1912. COURTESY OF THE WISCONSIN HISTORICAL SOCIETY, WHI-44529.

Carp by the Carload

The Queen of the Rivers

German immigrants to the Midwest lamented that none of the fish in America were as tasty as their beloved carp back home. A German friend told me about a yuletide carp swimming in her family's bathtub in East Germany; she couldn't bathe until the fish was filleted on Christmas Eve. To remedy the dearth of carp in their new home, "German and Scandina-vian immigrants helped stage a national letter write-in campaign to Congress to convince the senators to bring carp to the Midwest," University of Minnesota fisheries professor Peter Sorensen told me. "The carp arrived at Union Station in downtown St. Paul under guard because they were thought to be so valuable."

In Europe, carp were viewed along with trout as one of the best and most delicious game fish. Izaak

Just south of Stillwater, Minnesota, on the St. Croix River, this commercial fishing operation hauled in loads of large fish in 1914 that would leave modern anglers amazed. COURTESY OF THE MINNESOTA HISTORICAL SOCIETY.

Walton wrote in *The Compleat Angler*, "The Carp is the Queen of Rivers: a stately, a good, and a very subtle fish." Some years before in *Hamlet*, Shakespeare used carp as a synonym for a prize when Polonius tells Reynaldo to trick his son Laertes by saying, "Your bait of falsehood takes this carp of truth."

In 1877, the U.S. Commission of Fish and Fisheries intended to improve on nature by bringing 450 German carp across the Atlantic Ocean on a steamer and then breeding and distributing them. Because the carp were considered so valuable and beautiful, "Some were stocked in the reflecting pools in Washington, D.C.," Sorensen said.

Meanwhile, the media rejoiced. The *New York Times* in 1881 published recipes for stuffed, stewed, and broiled carp. The New York Fish Commission declared in 1880 that carp was the "fresh water fish of the future." The U.S. Commission of Fish and Fisheries believed that carp would be "an inexpensive source of protein for the benefit of all Americans."

On November 17, 1888, the *St. Paul Daily Globe* ran a banner headline, "CARP BY THE CARLOAD: Brain Food Which Will Be Distributed throughout the Northwest." The tickled journalist announced that "Car 1 of the United States fish commission, loaded with a cargo of the finny tribe in embryo, reached the city yesterday morning. . . . St. Paul is the distributing point for three states [Minnesota, Wisconsin, and Dakota Territory] and the car is loaded with carp." The supervisor aboard the train, C. C. Lewis, announced: "We have about ten thousand carp and a few goldfish on board now, but when we started out we carried fully thirty thousand carp. We have had abundant opportunity to get rid of them, and at each stopping place we disposed of a large consignment of our wares." In other words, the commission had already seeded lakes and rivers in Ohio, Missouri, and Iowa on the way. "We send out twenty fish to each applicant, and in the course of two or three years they will BREED AND INCREASE ABUNDANTLY." The journalist was correct, as the carp took over the bottoms of lakes.

Soon advertisements ran for these prized fish, such as one in the *St. Paul Daily Globe* that same year. "The carp are well known . . . and will give satisfaction to all fish eaters in quality and price also. These carp are raised in spring water at Hansen's (Big Spring Carp Fisheries), Fort Snelling." To ensure that this giant shipment of carp to the Midwest was put to best use, the Minnesota Fish Commission distributed a flyer, "Carp and Carp Culture," to educate recipients of the small carp on getting them to grow and flourish. The notice warned, "Carp, like pigs, will stand much abuse, either will survive being kept in a mudhole, but it spoils the flavor of the meat of both. . . . Complaint is made sometimes that they taste of mud."

This problem derived because "the carp dig around in the bottom of the lakes and stir up all the muck while uprooting aquatic plants," according to Sorensen. "Farmers' fields drained directly into rivers and lakes at the time, and Minneapolis and St. Paul used to cart trash onto the frozen Mississippi so it would all 'disappear' once spring came. No one knew any better. All that fertilizer and phosphorous is now being dug up by the carp on the bottom as they remove the plants that stabilize everything. The lakes have been reengineered."

Less than ten years later, newspapers that once

heralded the arrival of carp referred to the carp as a terrible mistake. The northern Minnesota *Virginia Enterprise* ran a headline on March 19, 1897, calling them "Guerrilla Fish" and lamented, "The devotees of the rod and line assert that in many lakes, where carp have been placed, the catching of black and calico bass is rapidly becoming a thing of the past." In 1895, the *St. Paul Daily Globe* referred to the "German menace" infesting our waters, even though carp are originally from the Caspian Sea. The xenophobic article warned, "The German Carp . . . now the foreigner is nothing but a piscatorial pariah—an outcast in the world of waters. If the solemn word of fishermen can be taken as fact, the sooner he is totally exterminated and driven out of these waters the better. . . . [The carp] is no better than a red-handed assassin . . . the carp is a fraud. His flesh has a sour, earthy flavor, and is soft and flabby to a disgusting degree." Carp were suddenly unwanted, but no one could stop them. Even so, fishermen harvested five million pounds of carp up to 1950 on the upper Mississippi River, mostly to ship abroad.

Stocking Fish

What's under the Waves?

"We are unknowingly paying for the sins of our grandparents, while continuing down the same road,"

Sorensen warned in 2015. "Our past is coming back to haunt us." He's referring to the U.S. government stocking invasive species, especially carp, in lakes and rivers in the Midwest from 1880 to 1890. "With our encouragement, they thought they could improve on nature. Instead, this was one of the biggest mistakes ever made."

After bringing thirty thousand carp to the Midwest in 1888, the U.S. Commission of Fish and Fisheries was so pleased with how easily carp spread that supervisor C. C. Lewis proclaimed, "On our next trip we will bring trout, then whitefish, and in the early spring, shad." Most of these fish didn't survive. Furthering the dangerous experiment with our waterways in the 1880s, the Minnesota Fish Commission tried to introduce salmon into Red Lake, Otter Tail Lake, and Detroit Lake, and failed completely. Lake

This image from 1910 shows the Minnesota State Fish Hatcheries near Mounds Park in St. Paul. Experimental stocking of Atlantic salmon into city lakes and rainbow trout into city ponds failed miserably. Carp, on the other hand, were wildly successful. COURTESY OF THE MINNESOTA HISTORICAL SOCIETY.

By 1925, fish stocks had already begun to dwindle. Here members of the Izaak Walton League of America, named for the famed British piscator, attempt to restock lakes with small fry. COURTESY OF THE MINNESOTA HISTORICAL SOCIETY.

In 1890, the *Princeton Union* newspaper from Princeton, Minnesota, declared: "Have a Carp Pond! No farmer who has a pond or can have a pond on his place can afford to be without a carp pond." Just one decade later, the carp took over lakes and had to be seined out by the hundreds. COURTESY OF THE BIG STONE COUNTY HISTORICAL SOCIETY.

Minnetonka saw the introduction of twenty-five hundred salmon of different types, and the Mississippi River got eighty thousand shad; almost all the fish died within the first year.

"They stocked Lake Como with rainbow trout. They even brought Atlantic salmon to Minneapolis lakes, and they all died, of course," Sorensen said. "It was driven by a democratic ethic," which essentially meant that citizens who made a fuss pushed the Minnesota Department of Natural Resources to stock the lakes. "DNR fisheries is largely funded by fishing licenses, so they necessarily cater to recreational fishermen."

By 1909, the Minnesota Game and Fish Commission wanted the carp out. Licensed contractors seined (netted) infected lakes to remove carp and other rough fish and then sold them out east or in Chicago. This proved reasonably effective, but they realized that carp would never be eradicated this way. The DNR eventually attempted "rough fish control," but success proved elusive as the production of young carp, the cause of it all, was not addressed. In the 1960s, the Minnesota Conservation Department promoted better living through chemistry and used the poison rotenone to kill all the fish in a lake. Between 1962 and 1968, this "total mortality" tactic was used in seventy-nine Minnesota lakes, followed by restocking to rebuild the ecosystem. Degraded wetlands support carp reproduction because they lack native predatory fish such as northern pike. Sorensen and his group recently discovered that common carp can on some occasions be controlled by restoring the wetlands to support the fish who prey on young carp, and then locating and removing adult carp when they

aggregate. A decade of basic science was required to figure this out.

Sorensen described the DNR's efforts at rough fish control "a disaster" since the carp survived and continue to thrive. He pointed out that we have a new carp problem: "The U.S. Fish and Wildlife Service working with other agencies later brought in Asian carp as well. They now threaten the Mississippi River ecosystem by feeding in the open water where common carp do not. It seems we did not learn much from the common carp." He explained how "Chicago dredged out the marsh in town, built a canal, and reversed the flow of the [Chicago] river to get rid of sewage and garbage around 1900. Zebra mussels came in this way. Now we risk getting Asian carp in the Great Lakes as well. Payback, I suppose." A proposed eighteen-billion-dollar project to cut off the Chicago River to prevent Asian carp might stop the spread, but DNA from these fish has allegedly been discovered in other tributary rivers to Lake Michigan. Sorensen suspects that people who like Asian carp have already put them in the lake, but it is not known if they will breed successfully.

Sorensen pointed out, "The DNR often lacks precise estimates of the numbers of fish in the lakes because it's hard and very expensive to figure it out. Estimates are generally based on netting that is conducted every few years to garner relative numbers, and Minnesota does better than most places." One problem is that these surveys don't usually show how many nongame fish are in the lake, and "sometimes the lakes are more than half carp." Their focus is generally on game fish, which is what most anglers want. "As scientists, we are interested in the entire lake and overall balance, to get a sample and discover what fish, including natives and exotics, are in the lakes," Sorensen said. "We put radio tags on the carp and let them go. They're called 'Judas fish' because they give away the other fish. Then we net them." His crew seines fish under the ice during the depths of winter. He described under-ice fishing with seine nets as a dying art—all these fishermen are in their fifties to seventies. "We seine about a third of a lake and pull it up through the ice. Thousands, no, tens of thousands of fish. We have some time to sort them out because it's so cold. We don't throw back the carp or the bullheads." This is expensive, but Sorensen and his team are then able to understand and in many cases improve lake ecosystems for long-term benefits.

Common carp are often the most abundant fish in the waters of the upper Midwest, "usually more than fifty percent of the biomass of fish in the lake," said Sorensen. On Lake Susan near Chanhassen, Minnesota, the DNR did a survey in 2009 that doesn't list any carp because the fish likely eluded the gill and trap nets. During the winter, Sorensen seined the lake, essentially taking all the fish, and discovered a massive amount of these bottom feeders. "We removed carp from Lake Susan, and the sunfish population got nice and big." In many lakes today, he said, "Sunfish are often out of balance, seemingly because fishers are taking all the bigger predatory fish. Darwin tells you that evolutionary pressure will prevail, so many fish, including sunfish, now appear to mature at smaller sizes and may be coming to dominate."

After his group removed the carp from Lake Susan, they did a creel survey to find out how many fish the anglers were taking. In one year, 70 to 80 percent of the fish were caught. "That's not a great scenario, but once someone catches a lot of fish, they get on their social network and soon everyone is there," said Sorensen. "Because of this, the lakes often get overfished or fished to the point where small fish dominate."

President Herbert Hoover made sarcastic comments about the impossibility of limiting anglers: "The Declaration of Independence is firm that all men—and boys—are endowed with unalienable rights, which obviously include the pursuit of fish." Prized fish have strict limits, and catch and release is encouraged, but carp have no limit on the number that can be taken. Perhaps this is one reason why *In-Fisherman* magazine declared that carp would soon be recognized as "the world's greatest sportfish."

Professor Sorensen emphasized, "Stocking is often not a great idea from a holistic perspective, but that, of course, depends on your objective. It's not always a good idea because you're introducing something that isn't native to the lake. Often stocked fish don't reproduce, so they need to keep stocking. It's not always self-sustaining and ends up costing a great deal—up to five dollars for a [grown-up] fish. It would be better for all—and the environment— to be self-sustaining with catch and release to keep the large fish and live with the environment. Fish, if given a chance, have an enormous capacity to grow quickly and reproduce prolifically. We see evidence of this in the stories our grandparents tell of catching huge and abundant fishes; these are not myths but rather reflect what our lakes are truly capable of." Stocking also risks moving invasive species and diseases around inadvertently. Still, an increasing number of anglers push to keep their catch and to have their lakes regularly stocked with game fish. Who doesn't want to take home a trophy?

In 1874, the Minnesota Fish Commission thought northern pike were a "calamity" that should be "outlawed" and was "fully convinced that every pickerel of the state simply occupies the room of better fish." Sorensen disagrees and thinks that we should try to return to the original makeup of the lakes and stop moving fish to different lakes. "I look at our native fishes, including pike, as beautifully and perfectly adapted machines, and now we're often moving them around to different environments. It's like putting a Chihuahua at the North Pole." Sorensen advocates for a balanced, sustainable approach while acknowledging the diverse interests involved. "One size does not fit all in nature. It is difficult, but not rocket science."

The losing battle of Jonah the Fisherman was immortalized in this painting. PIETER LASTMAN, *JONAH AND THE WHALE*, 1621. OIL ON OAK PANEL, 36 × 52 CM. STIFTUNG MUSEUM KUNSTPALAST, DÜSSELDORF.

Fishing Phenomena

Suffering Sea Serpents!

Landlubbers may discount the fantastic stories of gigantic underwater serpents as hogwash, but even the beginning of Genesis mentions the monsters from the deep: "So God created the great sea creatures . . . with which the waters swarm. . . . And God saw that it was good." Who would dare question the Bible?

On the other hand, an argument for evolution could be made with sightings of fish growing feet. *Fishing for Buffalo* tells how "even today, farmers on the Skunk River in Iowa tell tales of massive flathead catfish that crawl up from the river on hot nights to feed in the cornfields like deer." Freshwater fish are capable of remarkable feats, but crawling? The authors of that book claim that the remarkable and ubiquitous "bullhead needs little more than a mud puddle to survive." In other words, they could almost survive on land. In *North American Freshwater Fishing* author Mike Rosenthal writes that when he was little, he "dug bullheads from dry pond bottoms that looked like a huge puzzle of cracked earth. Under those conditions the fish were in the center of large lumps of dried mud. When the lump was opened it was similar to breaking an egg; each bullhead had constructed a small cell slightly larger than its body and lined with a mucus-like substance from the skin of the fish. . . . When dropped into water these bullheads immediately swam away, apparently unharmed by many weeks without water."

PORK IS GOING DOWN

If a mad beast from the deep could gobble up little piggies, imagine what it could do to little humans dipping toes in the water from the dock. COLLECTION OF DONALD HARRISON.

This isn't an isolated incident. In 1972 Richard Hagstrom wrote to the Dear Abby column: "I had a farm three miles from Ashland, Wisconsin. A storm broke suddenly, and afterward I saw tiny little fish in the cow tracks around our barn." *Scientific American* reported another strange episode in Combined Locks, Wisconsin, in which a woman who lived about fifteen hundred feet uphill from the Fox River found fresh fish, silver shiners about five inches long, on her driveway. With her son, she went out to search for more and found five more fish scattered around her property. The next day, she discovered five more on her lawn and even three on the roof. There are bizarre stories of large, "dark, fishing spiders" sighted in rural Wisconsin in 2014, according to the *Green Bay Press-Gazette*. These arachnids reach three inches in diameter and set traps to nab small fish or tadpoles for supper. The sightings have been confirmed by an expert in spiders, Michael Draney, from the University of Wisconsin–Green Bay.

Some of these stories may be plausible, but what about all the sightings of sea monsters in the lakes? Perhaps these are just fish tall tales, or, as President

Who knows if anyone actually believed this trick photography, but tall tales of attacking fish are widespread. COLLECTION OF DONALD HARRISON.

Herbert Hoover wrote, "Fishermen are gregarious. Otherwise, the mighty deeds of the day or of a year ago or of ten years ago would go unsung. No one but fishermen will listen to them." Perhaps an unsurprising detail of the stories is that the fish (or the monster) grows in size with each retelling.

In 1922, witnesses saw a beast that is hard to imagine even fitting into Michigan's Paint River where it was spotted. The creature had a "head bigger than a pail and about six humps sticking out of the water," according to *The Field Guide to Lake Monsters, Sea Serpents, and Other Mystery Denizens of the Deep*. The witness said, "It was swimming north up the river between two bridges. This distance could be the length of a city block, and this monster must have been nearly half of that bridge, but we followed its wake on up the river."

Beautiful Madison, Wisconsin, wedged between three lakes, is known for its student pranks. Not a vicious beast, the town's sea serpent in Lake Mendota was playful and nicknamed Bozho. The creature pranked swimmers and canoers by trailing their boats or tickling toes that dangled from docks—or was that just the sunfish? "Back in 1899, a group of ladies had spotted Bozho. . . . They reported that the

HOW WE DO THINGS AT CRAPO, MICH.

LANDING A PIKE
COPR 1910 BY AS JOHNSON JR
WAUPUN WIS.

From Michigan to Minnesota, tall-tale photography often found fishermen at odds with their revenge-seeking prey.
COLLECTION OF DONALD HARRISON.

serpent's head, which reared some distance out of the water, was ten inches in diameter and that the end of its tail, decorated with two big horns, lashed the water into a frothy foam as the creature dove beneath the waves," according to *Weird Wisconsin*. Then the sea serpent turned cruel, according to an angler in 1917, who reported that it had a "large snake-like head, with large jaws and blazing eyes." Perhaps this was a relative of the sister serpent across the isthmus in Lake Monona, where during the summer of 1897 a dog was missing after swimming and residents thought it had been eaten. A couple of days later, Eugene Heath, who worked at the Garr-Scott Company, fired his rifle at a "twenty-foot serpent plying the waters." Or perhaps that was his excuse for shooting firearms in town after a night at the bars.

The sightings follow a familiar pattern and often reflect early drawings of dragons. At Elkhart Lake in Wisconsin in the 1890s, a "creature with 'big jaws' and 'flashing eyes'" yanked a poor fisherman "end over end" into the lake. According to *Sea Monsters* by Charles E. Brown, a fifty-foot-long sea serpent spotted in Red Cedar Lake, Wisconsin, in 1891 had a "very large head with protuberances like saw teeth on its back." In 1890, tourists at another Wisconsin hot

A fight with a mad Pickrel.

Copyright 1911 by W.H.Martin.

This postcard from 1911 shows a mad pickerel getting revenge on a poor fisherman. PHOTOGRAPH BY W. H. MARTIN. COURTESY OF THE MINNESOTA HISTORICAL SOCIETY.

spot, Pewaukee Lake, reported a "huge green thing traveling like a gray streak" near the resorts along the shore. When the beast was attacked with a spear, the "weapon bounded back as though it had struck a rock or iron plate."

Even when witnesses are confronted with the impossibility of what they saw, they tend to stick by their story. During the summer of 1879 at Stump Pond at the Du Quoin fairgrounds in Illinois, a man fishing at night saw a creature making a huge wake that rocked his boat, so he refused to venture out again in the dark. The next year in July 1880, two miners saw a twelve-foot-long lake serpent with its "body the thickness of a telegraph pole and dark-green in color," according to *The Field Guide to Lake Monsters*. Over the years, new reports surfaced about the creature in the pond, and then in 1964 the little lake was drained and its "fish cleared out with electric stunners. The largest fish weighed thirty pounds." Even so, witnesses refused to believe it. "One of them was

Serpent Lake in northern Minnesota has never had sightings of mysterious beasts in the water. Instead, the winding lake is shaped like a serpent, so the nearby town of Crosby raised this colorful statue to the lake's namesake. AUTHOR'S PHOTOGRAPH.

NO CLIMBING ALLOWED

sixty-six-year-old Allyn Dunmeyer, whose boat had been nearly tipped over by something that had struck its bottom several years before. . . . 'I've seen them so near the surface that their back fins were sticking out of the water,'" he told the magazine *Fate* in 1965.

The biggest sea serpent sightings are reserved for the biggest lakes. The *Chicago Tribune* reported on August 7, 1867, "Lake Michigan is inhabited by a vast monster, part fish and part serpent." The reporter confirmed the existence of the creature due to two separate sightings, from the tugboat *George W. Wood* and from the propeller boat *Sky Lark.* The sightings were outside Evanston, Illinois, and the next day a fisherman, Joseph Muhike, sighted it again in the water off Hyde Park in Chicago. According to *The Field Guide to Lake Monsters,* the creature measured "between forty and fifty feet long and had a neck as thick as a human being's and body as thick as a barrel."

Even the earliest surviving book on fishing by Oppian of Cilicia from the second century declares that fishermen "shudder at the terrors awful to behold of the grim sea, even the Sea-monsters which encounter them when they traverse the secret places of the deep."

Crime with Extra Lines

The Revenge of Billy Bass

"Lots of people committed crimes during the year who would not have done so if they had been fishing," proclaimed President Herbert Hoover, pushing his sport so that many would become perfectly pure and angelic individuals. If only all fishermen were so innocent. Ironically, later in Hoover's fishing book he tells the apocryphal tale of asking a boy where he caught his beautiful fish and being told: "You just walk down that lane marked 'Private' till you come to a sign saying 'Trespassers Will Be Prosecuted.' Just beyond is a stream marked 'No Fishing Allowed,' and there you are." Is the president telling us we need to bend the rules to catch the best fish? Even Izaak Walton's book on fishing, *The Compleat Angler,* is dedicated "especially to the honest angler," insinuating that another kind of angler exists.

Historically, fishermen have not been so peaceful, and fishing waters have often been violently protected. British ships rammed Icelandic vessels during the vicious Cod Wars between 1958 and 1976. Japan and China had it out in the 1930s during the Cuttlefish Feud over who gets the most squid. Native Americans push for their treaty rights in the United States and are often met with stiff resistance, such as during the fish wars in the Pacific Northwest in the 1960s and 1970s. The Food and Agriculture Organization of the United Nations estimated in 2014 that twenty billion dollars of illegal fishing takes place each year in the world. Most of the infractions in the north woods are not as contentious.

Many begin with anglers who are out to trick fish and figure they can trick the sheriff, too. Minnesota conservation officer Curt Rossow wrote about nabbing many of these deviant fishermen, most of the time for the relatively minor offense of leaving a fishing line unattended. One of the lawbreakers rebutted, "There are no fish in the lake; it's not like I was trying to catch anything." One irate, but guilty,

When Al Capone wasn't evading his income tax responsibilities or planning a Valentine's Day gift to some wise guys, he took time to fish in his pajamas from his boat, as shown here in a photograph from 1940. Capone had a fishing hideaway of more than four hundred acres in northern Wisconsin in the town of Couderay; the house had eighteen-inch-thick walls to protect him from machine-gun fire. Perhaps that scar on his face came from an errant hook destined for a muskie. PHOTOGRAPH FROM ASSOCIATED PRESS: COPYRIGHT AP IMAGES.

angler "threatened to set his German shepherd on me! I told him that if he did that, I'd have to shoot his dog!" Another time Rossow grabbed a bobber in the middle of a lake that was dipping up and down in the water. "I pulled a nice bullhead in (if there is such a thing as a nice bullhead)." The line led all the way to a dock and a rod and reel and the offender in his house. Later in the summer, Rossow was in his boat near the shore and noticed one of the earlier deviant fishermen. "He saw us, bent over, and mooned us!"

He did encounter more serious fishing criminals, such as the poacher who arrived on his bike at the lake with a gill net to fill his boat. When the bicycle fish thief stepped on shore, Rossow tried to arrest him. Instead, the culprit "immediately jumped in his boat and started throwing fish back into the lake!" Rossow grabbed him from the boat intending to handcuff him, but they began wrestling as the man's dog chomped on Rossow's leg. The officer finally punched the lawbreaker and got him into the squad car, only to discover that they had been wrestling in cow manure.

Illegally netted fish often sell for three dollars a pound, versus ten dollars retail, and often end up at community fish fries rather than restaurants. The *Minneapolis Star Tribune* reported on May 3, 2013, about the recent history of banned netting on Red Lake. Greg Spaulding, a Minnesota Department of Natural Resources conservation officer who retired in

2007 after twenty-seven years, said, "In the early '80s we found piles of fish carcasses three feet high and twenty feet across on the shores of Red Lake. That booty, combined at the time with walleye poaching by sport anglers, contributed to the collapse of Red Lake walleyes in the mid-1990s." Another DNR conservation officer, Mike Hruza, who retired in 2010, added, "We used to pull nets out of Red Lake that had a ton of dead fish in them. The fish that came off Red Lake illegally had to add up to millions of pounds." Both thought it would be very difficult to conclusively stop the illegal fish trade in the north woods. The DNR staged a massive sting operation in Lake of the Woods along the Canadian border, and the *St. Paul Pioneer Press* reported in January 2014 that forty DNR conservation officers seized evidence

The Wisconsin Conservation Commission issued fishing licenses and promoted the great outdoors to avid anglers in times of both war and peace.

WISCONSIN
FISHING
LAWS
1944

A DURATION PLEDGE
I WILL DO MY PART TO CONSERVE
WISCONSIN WOODS, WATERS
AND WILDLIFE;
I WILL DO MY UTMOST
SPORTSMAN'S DUTY TO KEEP
OUR OUTDOORS GLORIOUS;
I PLEDGE TO ACCEPT THIS TRUST
UNTIL LASTING PEACE
IS EARNED
AND THOSE THAT ARE GONE
COME HOME!

HELP PREVENT FOREST FIRES

of several fishing guides violating limits on walleyes as well as "illegal bear guiding activity."

Most illicit fishing incidents tend to be rather banal, even comical. For example, a Long Island man was determined to start a personal aquarium in his living room and began gathering fish. He entered a pet store in an overcoat, reached into a 250-gallon fish tank and pulled out a baby nurse shark. He stuffed the foot-long carnivore under his jacket and nonchalantly walked out of the store, dripping water in his wake. The *New York Daily News* ran an article titled "Shark and Awe Heist" about the bizarre theft. The crook followed up the shark theft by buying an enormous moray eel on a stolen credit card to provide company for his stolen shark. Perhaps he didn't read up on these creatures, but certain species of moray eels can grow nine feet long and the shark up to fourteen feet. Also, these sharks eat eels.

Another bumbling crook burgled a bait shop in Rochester, Minnesota, in search of loot but probably not minnows. The owner of the Hooked on Fishing shop had placed a Big Mouth Billy Bass on the door. The intruder triggered the motion sensor when the novelty fish fell to the floor. The animatronic toy belted out the lyrics to "Take Me to the River," according to Sgt. Tom Claymon of the Olmsted County Sheriff's Office as reported in the *Minneapolis Star Tribune* on February 4, 2014. Even though a wad of cash was sitting in "a very visible spot," the thief was spooked by Billy Bass and skedaddled. Sergeant Claymon reported that the burglar didn't take anything, and the heroic fish "took one for the team. There were plenty of things to take but nothing was missing . . . other than Billy's pride."

World Capital® Wars
Fishing Towns Fight

For once, the Minnesota Legislature was nearly unanimous when declaring that the walleye was the official state fish in 1965, but some spoilsport (who was probably stumping for the bullhead) voted "nay" in the 128 to 1 tally. In reverence of the lunkers hooked in its waters, Garrison, Minnesota, on Lake Mille Lacs, was soon nominated the "Walleye Capital of the World."

Not so fast, warned Baudette, Minnesota, which also claimed the title. Many other towns declared for themselves the prominent honor of producing these delicious fish: Ray, Minnesota; Rush City, Minnesota; Bays de Noc, Michigan; Mobridge, South Dakota; Umatilla, Oregon; and Shell Lake, Wisconsin, which now stays out of the fracas by referring to itself simply as "Walleye Country" and has a strange statue of a mutant walleye with two tails to prove it.

The *Bismarck Tribune* pushed to keep the walleye capital in Garrison, North Dakota, but quoted Fred Snyder from Ohio State University, who insisted that Port Clinton, Ohio, on Lake Erie, was the special spot. "There is no other body of water that produces the poundage per acre of walleye that Lake Erie does," the professor boasted. Impressively, the town celebrates New Year's Eve not with a ball drop but by lowering its eighteen-foot walleye, named Captain Wylie, from a crane. A new Junior Miss Walleye is crowned each year as royalty for this "Walleye Madness at Midnight."

In 2007, Baudette challenged all these other newcomers and tried to trademark the title "Walleye Capital of the World." Incredibly, the state of

Alongside Minnesota governor Karl Rolvaag (*right*), the state's best-known wildlife artist, Roger Preuss (*center*), presented Iowa governor Harold E. Hughes with the first official State Fish print in Ely, circa 1965. Preuss's wily wall-eye appeared on thousands of postcards during the 1960s.
COURTESY OF THE MINNESOTA HISTORICAL SOCIETY.

MINNESOTA STATE FISH

On the shores of Lake Mille Lacs, the town of Isle, Minnesota, erected a sculpture staking its claim as the "Walleye Capital of the World." PHOTOGRAPH BY THE AUTHOR.

Decals from Baudette and Big Falls, Minnesota, continue the debate over which northwoods fishing haven is the true home of the walleyed pike. AUTHOR'S COLLECTION.

Minnesota played favorites and awarded Baudette the trademark for ten years. The town then filed for a federal trademark and had to wade through mounds of bureaucracy from the U.S. Patent and Trademark Office, which requested information about how Baudette would use the title. The *Minneapolis Star Tribune* reported in 2007 that the trademark would give Baudette "the right to tell other towns to back off. Indeed, it would give the bureau the right to sue in federal court to prevent unauthorized use of the trademark." The newspaper quoted Gregg Hennum of the Lake of the Woods Tourism Bureau: "We don't want to create any enemies. But it's business." In 2015, I checked the status of the application with the receptionist at the Lake of the Woods Tourism Bureau. "We officially got the recognition about five years ago," she responded proudly. As far as the other towns that still use the nickname "Walleye Capital of the World," she told me, "They might call themselves that but they don't get to use the trademark logo."

Even if a town holds that title officially, it's questionable how it can be enforced. Boulder Junction, Wisconsin, succeeded in establishing the U.S. trademark as the "Musky Capital of the World," but Hayward, Wisconsin, calls itself the same thing, as does Leech Lake, Minnesota, and Lake of the Woods, which stretches from northern Minnesota into Ontario. To further inflame passions, assemblyman Willis Hutnik from the Hayward area introduced legislation in 1955 to the Wisconsin state legislature to make the muskie the official state fish. In the proposal, he mentioned that Hayward is the muskie capital of the world without knowing that Boulder Junction officially held that title. "Incensed by this shameless disregard for their legally secured right to exclusive use of the title, the folk of Boulder Junction rallied together," explains the website of the town of Boulder Junction. Even though Hayward claims the largest muskie ever caught, Boulder Junction dismisses this as nonsense and contends, "The 'Musky Capital' tag has always been premised on the total number of Muskies caught, not the size of one freak fish."

To resolve the issue once and for all, Representative Ellsworth Gaulke from Lac du Flambeau introduced legislation in 1971 to the Wisconsin legislature to strike the offhand mention of Hayward as a muskie capital from the official record. The *Milwaukee Journal* on March 9, 1971, reported on how state legislators pass their time and quoted in detail: "In 1955 a misguided, chauvinistic, and overzealous state representative, who shall remain nameless, had the unmitigated gall to introduce a joint resolution which with a certain low cunning referred to the city of Hayward, a blameless community which was led astray by these machinations in Madison, as the 'muskie capital of the world' (lower case)." The joint resolution that passed in 1955 "has stuck in the craw of the good people and gentle folk of Boulder Junction like a dratted salmon bone." The new formal proposal asks "that this blemish be removed, this blot erased, this mote in the eye of Boulder Junction be hereby and forthwith exorcised . . . revoked, expunged, repealed, and dead as any mackerel." Even so, citizens of Hayward refer to their town as the "Muskie Capital of the World" (or sometimes diplomatically as the "Muskie Capital of Wisconsin"). And going far beyond some little trademark symbol, Hayward built a 145-foot-long Muskie to prove its point.

Female Fish Impersonators

Cuckolds and Fakers

Sirens of the sea tempt sailors and fishermen far from home. Disgruntled "fishing widows" are left behind and become more bitter when the fishing opener falls on Mother's Day weekend. Perhaps fishing is simply better than sex, or as actor Clark Gable put it, "Hell, if I'd jumped on all the dames I'm supposed to have jumped on, I'd have had no time to go fishing." Minnesota fisherman Geoff Johnson told me about his fellow anglers who can't resist being in the boat:

Amorous fishing couples wed in the mouth of the beast overlooking Hayward Lake. To secure its claims as "Muskie Capital of the World," Hayward, Wisconsin, built a giant Leaping Muskie measuring half a block long. PHOTOGRAPH COURTESY OF JACOB KREJCI.

"These guys are serious. Lotsa real bad marriages and really good fishermen." Is there some sort of carnal allure to fishing? Strangely, *Marie Claire* and other news sources claim that an antiquated Minnesota law warns that it is illegal for any man to have sexual intercourse with a live fish.

Is there an erotic lure of fishing? "It was in this way that I came across the first visual image of a seminaked woman that I had ever seen," remembers Australian art critic Robert Hughes in *A Jerk on One End.* "It was not a photograph. It was molded, in clear Lucite, on the spool on which an American

Smooth

Smooth casting and smooth reeling! That's the new Rain-Beau Nyline, the most perfect fly line ever built. Made of Dupont Nylon, its extra flexibility and fine tapers give it casting qualities superior to any line you've ever known.

Nyline comes with double taper, tear-drop taper or level, beautifully oil finished in amber or mahogany with a waterproof, easily dressed, non-peeling surface that stands unusual abuse. Fill your reel with Nyline and see how much easier accurate casting can be.

Ask your dealer about other Rain-Beau Lines of nylon, silk, linen, cotton and bronze. There is one for every fishing purpose, priced to fit your purse.

RAIN-BEAU
fishing lines

LINEN   COTTON   NYLON   SILK   BRONZE

Every Rain-Beau Nyline is put up on the unique crystal-clear plastic Rain-Beau coiler that makes drying and rewinding a cinch.

RAIN-BEAU PRODUCTS CO., CANTON, MASS., Division of INTERNATIONAL BRAID Co., PROVIDENCE, R. I.

75

fly-fishing line had been coiled . . . made in some place called Milwaukee, far away in unimaginable America. Lucky Americans, to have such things on fishing gear!"

All the way back in the second century, Oppian of Cilicia guessed that some salacious intrigue unfolded under the waves when he wrote, "All that inhabit the watery flood and where each dwells, their mating in the waters and their birth, the life of fishes, their hates, their loves, their wiles." Now scientists are beginning to discover the extent of the sexual chicanery of fish.

In 2001, Erik Petersson and Torbjorn Järvi, scientists at Sweden's National Board of Fisheries, studied the mating habits of brown trout and discovered that the females tricked the males by quivering intensely with their mouths open to fake orgasm. The males released their sperm and often the females held back their eggs so they could move on in search of true love with a more hulky mate. The snooping scientists watched 134 couples and observed 69 times that the females tricked the males into ejaculating prematurely. "The females behave as if they should spawn," Järvi told *New Scientist*. "They trick the males into releasing their sperm." Ironically, the females often returned to these males if they couldn't find a better suitor.

Male largemouth bass won't put up with this. They are extremely aggressive and attack "just about anything swimming by that might remotely be a

Models trying their luck with a fishing pole were often featured in tackle advertising like this 1946 advertisement for Rain-Beau Fishing Lines.

threat, including scuba divers monitoring nests!" according to Robert Zink in *The Three-Minute Outdoorsman*. The females prefer these belligerent males and will release more eggs with these macho fish. The only problem is these combative fish also pounce on any lure that comes near the nest and end up on someone's plate. Fortunately, open season on bass has been adjusted to allow these virile males to guard the eggs so that smaller bass don't weaken the gene pool.

Large male bluegills have a problem with pesky young males pretending to be female in order to sneak by the protective male. Once the coast is clear, the young bluegills quickly copulate with the female fish behind the unsuspecting mate's back. "Sunfish pursue alternative strategies in which males mimic females to steal mates from other males," according to fisheries professor Peter Sorensen at the University of Minnesota. The sneaky schemes of these philandering Don Juans is appropriately known as an ART, or "alternative reproductive tactic," according to an article in *Biology Letters* from 2007. Known as "cuckolders," since they make a cuckold out of the unattentive male mates, these adolescent "sneaker males" often have female color patterns on their bodies that let them slip by the older males who are guarding their mates. These lascivious young bluegills even cross over to mate with female pumpkinseed sunfish, but young pumpkinseed males have started using this same trick to impregnate older female fish.

According to Matt Walker in *Fish That Fake Orgasms*, "These weedy, sneaky males have a trick up their sleeve that gives them a head start over their larger, more thuggish competitors: they produce physiologically superior sperm that swim faster." In other words, their female mimicry is just one of their secrets to get the gal. These acts account for almost 25 percent of bluegill mating, so Sorensen worries that all the big sunfish might be caught by fishers. "If we remove all large males, we could be shifting populations to these smaller mimic males." And all we'd be left with are these duplicitous little seducers. ❧

Keep your fish on ice! In 1959 an intrepid family braved the ice of Minnesota's Lake Mille Lacs for a day of walleye fishing.
PHOTOGRAPH BY THOMAS J. ABERCROMBIE / NATIONAL GEOGRAPHIC CREATIVE.

CHAPTER THREE

Beyond Angling
From Ice Fishing to Dynamite

Angling or float fishing I can only compare to a stick and a string, with a worm at one end and a fool at the other.

—English writer Samuel Johnson, circa 1750

Most fishing consists of trolling or casting off the dock on beautiful northern lakes or even flying in to remote lakes in Canada. But what about other ways of capturing the creatures from the deep? Unique to the frozen north is ice fishing. Who would believe we drive trucks on ice to place little heated houses above frozen water?

Over millennia, hungry fishers have experimented with many techniques to outwit the fish. One approach requires a late-night rendezvous on a lazy river: spearing suckers. Pull on rubber hip boots, grab a trident spear (just like Neptune), and strap on a battery-powered headlamp. Wade knee-deep through a stream in search of supper by harpooning some poor suckers hiding below the current.

Fly-fishing is perhaps the most technically difficult form of putting fish on the dinner table. Far beyond paying to wet a line in a stocked trout pond, river fly-fishing involves dedication and outfoxing the wily brook trout and other such species.

Fishing for steelhead trout also calls for dedication to nab these spawning fish early in the spring when they venture from the Great Lakes up rivers to lay their eggs. As soon as the ice opens up, these trout travel upstream only to be met by insistent fishermen.

Hand fishing, or "noodling," essentially uses the fisherman's arm as bait as he (almost all of them are men) wiggles his hand into an old muskrat den that has been taken over by catfish. The giant fish envelops his whole fist in its mouth, then the fisherman grabs the gills and struggles to bring the bottom-feeder to the surface. The danger of losing fingers or accidentally discovering an angry muskrat rather than a flathead catfish adds a little more risk to the venture.

When all else fails, lazy anglers resort to the highly illegal and destructive method of dynamiting for dinner.

Riding Sturgeon

King of the Fishes

Henry Wadsworth Longfellow waxed poetic about the largest freshwater fish in North America in his famous poem "Song of Hiawatha":

> On the white sand of the bottom
> Lay the monster, Mishe-Nahma
> Lay the sturgeon, king of Fishes.

The Ojibwe likely recognized the power of these giant sturgeons that often live longer than humans and can grow larger, up to three hundred pounds. "Among the northwoods Ojibwe, the lake sturgeon figured as *Na-me*, one of the most powerful spirits, the water dweller who orchestrated the movements of other water beings and who determined humans' success on the water roads," according to Jan Zita Grover in *Northern Waters*. Even so, the Ojibwe wove "sturgeon racks" from branches and basswood cords and would corral the giant fish into a smaller and smaller area and then kill them with clubs.

Out east in "earliest Virginia" the Native Americans who were part of the Powhatan Confederacy had a risky way of catching sturgeon, like a rodeo star. John McPhee wrote in *The Founding Fish*, "A cockarouse was any Pamunkey [named for someone along the Pamunkey River] who could wade into the river and cinch a noose over a sturgeon's tail, and then hang on, even if the sturgeon hauled him under water, and ultimately bring the fish to the riverbank."

When the French explorer Pierre-Esprit Radisson traveled through the Great Lakes in 1660, he wrote about frameworks the Native Americans set up on the south shore of Lake Superior to dry thousands of filleted sturgeon. A century later in 1767, Jonathon Carver ventured up the Mississippi and Minnesota Rivers and wrote about the Native Americans who speared sturgeon "as they lie under the banks in a clear stream, and darting at them with a fish-spear; for they will not take a bait."

Another hundred years later, when European settlers began netting fish across the north woods, they complained that these giant sturgeon spoiled their catch and ruined their nets. "In retaliation, commercial anglers killed every sturgeon they caught and either dumped them back to the rivers or fed the fish to pigs," according to *Fishing for Buffalo*. They chopped open the sturgeon and fed the eggs to pigs. The fishermen poured kerosene on piles of the giant

Paul Kane, *Fishing by Torch Light, Menominee*, portrays Native Americans spearfishing on the Fox River in Wisconsin. OIL ON CANVAS, 45.7 × 73.6 CM. THE HONOURABLE GEORGE WILLIAM ALLAN COLLECTION, ROYAL ONTARIO MUSEUM. GIFT OF SIR EDMUND OSLER. 912.1.10. REPRODUCED WITH PERMISSION OF THE ROYAL ONTARIO MUSEUM. COPYRIGHT ROM IMAGES.

deceased beasts and burned them, and "others were stacked on the decks of steamships and used to fire the boilers."

Many viewed them as a sort of sea monster. D. W. Seybert and Ed McKenzie were having a rowboat race on Rock Lake in Wisconsin in the late summer of 1882 when a large log floated close to the surface but then "manifested life" and lifted its "head about three feet out of the water," according to the book

Weird Wisconsin. "Strike him with the oar!" Seybert screamed, but McKenzie was too afraid to move and instead called to others on the beach. Captain Wilson ran to the shore with a shotgun, but the beast had already dived, and the air around it was "heavy with a most sickening odor."

However, sturgeon had been considered royal fish all the way back to Roman times. They were so prized by King Edward II that he proclaimed that all

This fisherman landed this giant sturgeon in 1925 in Warroad, Minnesota. Sturgeon could sometimes reach three hundred pounds—much more than the anglers who snagged them. COURTESY OF THE MINNESOTA HISTORICAL SOCIETY.

The old trick of posing kids next to a fish to make it look bigger isn't necessary with this 176-pound sturgeon that measured 87 inches. Instead of being snagged with a hook, this fish was "trapped" in White Earth Lake in 1926. COURTESY OF THE BECKER COUNTY HISTORICAL SOCIETY.

sturgeon were the property of the king: "The King shall have Wreck of the Sea throughout the Realm, Whales and (great) Sturgeons taken in the sea or elsewhere within the Realm." Prior to Edward, since King Henry I, sturgeon were to be eaten only at royal banquets.

When the fishermen on the Great Lakes realized how some cherished these fish and after they discovered the value of the eggs, a caviar plant was set up on Lake Erie in Sandusky, Ohio. The bladder of the fish was used to clarify wine and beer, and even the sturgeon skin was tanned as a sort of leather for shoes and purses. So many sturgeon were slaughtered that numbers plummeted. In Lake of the Woods, for example, the sturgeon population decreased 90 percent by 1900. Fisherman William Hjortsberg wrote in *Silent Seasons* that the prehistoric-looking paddlefish also took a hit, and most people will never see one. "Sturgeon are more numerous, but spreading caviar on toast is the closest most of us get to them."

Since a female doesn't lay eggs for her first twenty years, sturgeon have been slow to recover. If they are snagged, they must be let go in hopes of living for many more decades. The oldest sturgeon recorded was 152 years old in Lake of the Woods in 1953; most are forty to fifty years old. In April 1941, fisheries chief Hjalmar Swenson nabbed a 142-pound rock sturgeon, according to *Classic Minnesota Fishing Stories.* "After pictures, I attached a cattle tag #99 to the gill cover and turned the big fish loose." Now that the sturgeon are slowly making a comeback, perhaps some bold fisher will lasso one for a ride.

Early Commercial Fishing

No Road to the Port

The first Europeans to make it as far as the upper Midwest were the French voyageurs who established friendly trading relations with the Cree, Dakota, and Ojibwe in the area. They set up trade routes throughout the lakes and all the way to the Canadian Rockies. Before the pilgrims landed at Plymouth Rock in 1620, French explorers had traveled through Lake Superior.

In the 1830s, the fur trade fell into a slump because many of the animals had already been killed and styles in Europe were changing. Many of the old outposts were nearly abandoned, so John J. Astor's American Fur Company set up fishing stations at some of the unused sites in Minnesota at Grand Portage and in Wisconsin at Fond du Lac and its headquarters at La Pointe. Rather than relying on the French bateaux or their voyageur canoes, the company built a 111-ton schooner in 1835, named for the founder. The *John Jacob Astor* was the first of four ships to connect these sites and ship out nearly five thousand barrels of fish a year to the east. The fishermen—mostly Métis (mixed French and Indian blood) and French Canadians—caught one million pounds of fish in 1839. Coopers worked at the fish stations to construct barrels to haul the fish to Detroit, New Orleans, and New York. In 1842, the American Fur Company went belly up, and the fishing industry slumped. Still, some seasonal fishermen continued to net and then ship their catch out east.

Before the 1854 Treaty of La Pointe officially gave all the land in Minnesota's Arrowhead region

This haul from Lake Superior shows the giant fish that once populated the lake. PHOTOGRAPH BY PAUL GAYLORD, CIRCA 1885. COURTESY OF THE KATHRYN A. MARTIN LIBRARY, UNIVERSITY OF MINNESOTA DULUTH, ARCHIVES AND SPECIAL COLLECTIONS.

On the east side of Two Rivers, Wisconsin, is the historic French Side Fishing Village, part of which has been converted into a museum. The LeClair Fish Shed is a great example of fish houses used by early commercial fishermen on Lake Michigan. PHOTOGRAPH BY THE AUTHOR.

on Lake Superior's north shore to the United States, land cruisers were already illegally setting up claim shacks along the shore, convinced that the land would be valuable not only for fishing but for mineral rights. The Ojibwe tribes that signed the treaty would retain fishing rights, but as with many treaties, the settlers tried to reject those rights over the years.

Nearly ninety commercial fishermen fished Lake Superior in Lake County, Minnesota, in 1857. No road connected these fishing outposts, so steamboats made regular runs to exchange supplies for fish. By 1869, construction had begun on a railway in Duluth while steamboats connected the harbor with Chicago, Buffalo, and other cities on the Great Lakes. Despite the rosy predictions, the Panic of 1873 put the country into the "Great Depression," a term later attached to the market crash in the 1930s. Duluth's population withered to 1,300 residents in 1873, just a third of what it had been.

Trucks loaded with fresh catch from Samuel L. Goldish's Lake Superior Fish Company are stocked and ready for delivery to Duluth and the surrounding communities of northeastern Minnesota. PHOTOGRAPH CIRCA 1915. COURTESY OF THE KATHRYN A. MARTIN LIBRARY, UNIVERSITY OF MINNESOTA DULUTH, ARCHIVES AND SPECIAL COLLECTIONS.

Duluth's number of commercial fisherman dropped to 35 in 1879, but six years later there were 195. The Booth Packing Company in Duluth sent steamers all the way up the coast to Grand Portage to collect the catch. Three times a week from April to December, these early fishermen rowed their skiffs out to passing steamships in the "mosquito fleet," as they called them. These boats were their only connection to the outside world and brought salt, empty barrels, food, mail, and other provisions. At one point, the Booth Packing Company shipped one hundred tons of fresh fish per month to destinations as far away as St. Paul, St. Louis, Chicago, and Kansas City.

One of the best-known steamships was the *America*, which sank just off the southern edge of Isle Royale in 1928, with its forward deck and wheelhouse sticking out of the water until winter storms and ice sheared off the wheelhouse. It is now a popular wreck for diving.

Shoveling Herring

Scandinavians Net the Great Lakes

Forty years after the American Fur Company went bust, Scandinavians flooded into the area around the Great Lakes to revive commercial fishing and bring their skills to the waters of North America. The original fishing shacks, of which a few survive, are based on the *rorbuer* in Norway that are close to the water and perched on stilts in case waves sweep up to the building. Scandinavians often built the fish house first, which became "the receiving room and the shipping depot, the processing plant, and the executive

Before miracle nylon nets, commercial fishing colonies (such as this beautifully remote one on the Great Lakes) had to dry nets on these large spools so the line wouldn't decay. COURTESY OF THE KATHRYN A. MARTIN LIBRARY, UNIVERSITY OF MINNESOTA DULUTH, ARCHIVES AND SPECIAL COLLECTIONS.

office," according to the North Shore Commercial Fishing Museum. The boat could be wheeled right into the house to be unloaded while keeping out the cold wind. The second floor was the sleeping quarters where the family lived, and rope and nets were dried from the second-floor porch. Although fish houses were always near the lakeshore, later ones tended to be farther from the shore as lakeshore property became more valuable.

Lifting mounds of fresh lake herring, or ciscoes, by gripping the slippery fish would take hours. Herring shovels sped up the job. PHOTOGRAPH BY THE AUTHOR.

Washington Island, one of the notable fishing colonies on Lake Michigan, saw perhaps the first group of Icelanders in the United States and was one of the earliest immigrant settlements in the state when founded in 1865. The "Icelandic Castle" was built in 1875 to welcome new Scandinavian families to the area. A letter from Arni Gumundsen to relatives back in Iceland in 1872 said, "We believe that they were the first three Icelanders to come to America. . . . Now I have to tell you what we eat most here: wheat bread, butter, wheat porridge, pancakes, coffee, potatoes, very little meat, an unceasing flow of syrup, cabbage, turnips, bacon, fish, and so forth." Gumundsen longed for Icelandic lamb and other meat.

The seemingly endless supply of lake herring kept these new immigrants fed, so much so that the fishermen designed herring shovels to scoop the massive number of fish from the boats. According to the North Shore Commercial Fishing Museum, fisherman Ted Tofte recalled, "During one herring run in 1916, over two hundred 100-pound kegs of herring were caught, cleaned, and salted in the twin fish house in five days. . . . So ended the biggest herring run in my experience." The year before, 1915, was a boom year with almost ten thousand tons of fish sent to Duluth.

Many of the first Scandinavians paid for their relatives or friends to come to fish, but the newcomers would often have to work hard for two years to pay off the debt. Some complained that the owners of the fishing houses treated them like indentured servants. The conditions were often brutal. For example, to begin the fishing season as soon as possible on Isle Royale, fishermen often hauled their boats across the ice beginning in April to get to open water. The storms on the Great Lakes were swift and legendary. During one unforeseen storm in 1935, fishermen Carl Husebe and Christian Tveekrem from Thomasville didn't return for ten days and were finally discovered frozen stiff in their boat. According to the North

588. TORSKEHOVEDER

ENDRET: K KNUDSEN & CO A.S. BERGEN.

Across the Atlantic, mountains of *torskehoveder* (codfish heads) were shoveled onto the docks in Bergen, Norway, at the height of the commercial fisheries. PHOTOGRAPH BY KNUD KNUDSEN, 1885. COURTESY OF THE NATIONAL LIBRARY OF NORWAY.

When not on the water of the Great Lakes, commercial fishermen constructed herring boxes. Commercial fishers used handy metal stencils to efficiently make their mark on barrels and boxes. PHOTOGRAPHS BY THE AUTHOR.

Shore Commercial Fishing Museum, fishing had "one overriding advantage: the freedom of working for oneself"—although it could be deadly.

One fisherman was Swedish immigrant Charlie Nelson, who settled in Lutsen. He survived the early winters in large part because of the Ojibwe in the area, in particular White Sky and Jim Gesick, who supplied him with meat, taught him how to make maple syrup, and showed him where to find berries. In 1893, he added a second story to his fish house to host guests who came to visit him on the north shore of Lake Superior. Gradually, his home became a destination for paying visitors, and his income from hosting soon overtook that of fishing. In 1948, a ski area was added, since fishing tourism had dropped off.

Until 1929, no road ran north of Two Harbors on the north shore of Lake Superior in Minnesota, so fishing tourists who ventured to Lutsen, Grand Marais, and Hovland had to arrive via steamship. When Highway 61, which Bob Dylan sang about, eventually connected all these towns, "boxes of fresh fish were left along the highway to be picked up by 'fish trucks,'" according to the North Shore Commercial Fishing Museum, located along the highway in Tofte. Although commercial fishing weakened, tourism thrived. Poor fishermen could take advantage of the boom by renting cabins along the shore and selling the catch of the day. At the same time, recreational fishing flourished, and state legislatures passed laws that limited commercial fishing after extensive lobbying by recreational fishermen. By 1975 the number of commercial fishermen had dwindled to 137 versus almost 3,000,000 sport fishermen.

Noodling for Catfish

Just Stick Your Arm in a Log

Catfish will eat most anything. According to Sternberg's *The Art of Freshwater Fishing*, bait for catfish includes "congealed chicken blood, entrails of small animals, freshwater clams that have rotted in the sun for a day or two, dead birds, mice, frogs, worms, crayfish, grasshoppers, Limburger cheese, doughballs, and any number of homemade or commercially produced stinkbaits." Izaak Walton in his classic treatise on fishing from 1653 recommended the "flesh of a rabbit, or cat, cut small." A. George Morris, in *Sport Fishing USA*, wrote that the diet of catfish varies according to the season, but you can't go wrong with peanut butter, and "I even know one man who put half a jigger of his favorite booze in the dough. . . . He caught fish." The best bait for channel catfish, according to Morris, is a bar of white laundry soap. "One thing about using soap as a bait is that the fish caught will have clean mouths."

Even though fish farms raise more than three hundred million pounds of catfish each year, many prefer wild-caught fish even if they may have a muddy taste. One trick to preparing "off-flavored" catfish is to marinade chunks of the meat in lemon-lime soda for at least four hours or, better, overnight to remove any residue from its life in the muck.

Black bullheads are bottom-feeders and some of the strangest looking specimens ever. The sport of catfish "noodling" involves placing your fist inside the fish's mouth and latching hold of it—if the fish doesn't get hold of you first. PHOTOGRAPH BY ERIC ENGBRETSON. COPYRIGHT ENGBRETSON UNDERWATER PHOTOGRAPHY.

In the past, baiting a hole, or "chumming," was legal, and Morris recommended "canned corn (whole grain) or shelled corn that has been soaked. . . . If available, one cotton-seed cake should be planted on the bottom of the hole each week . . . more enjoyment than you ever realized possible." At Bay Lake in central Minnesota, Tame Fish Lake Road runs by Ruttger's Bay Lake Lodge and leads to Ak-Sar-Ben Gardens, which used to feature the two Vogt brothers dressed in overalls who would ring a bell at feeding time, and the fish would scoot over for a snack just like Pavlov's dog. The famous rock gardens and baited fish lured such celebrities as Will Rogers, Clark Gable, and Norma Talmadge but is now on private grounds. While baiting a hole is hardly very sporting, "noodling" is arguably one of the more courageous, if perhaps foolish, forms of fishing.

It all starts with love. Enamored male and female catfish court each other in the depths of a lake by massaging each other with their whiskers up and down their sleek bodies. These catfish literally taste each other—their thousands of taste buds rest not only in their whiskers but all over their fishy figures. It's true that a catfish can taste with its tail. They search for a love nest—anywhere hidden where they can lay eggs out of the reach of the predatory fish that seek to scuttle their relationship. An old tire, a log, a cavern made from a discarded plywood board, or a crack between rocks makes the perfect amorous rendezvous. The sweethearts wiggle each other's tails around their heads and quiver in delight. The inseminated eggs are released in this secret spot for the male to guard.

This is when the bravest fishers step in. The cat- fish viciously protect the nest, so daring noodlers dig around in the muck in search of the big fish. Also called "grabbling," "hogging," or "bulldogging," this bizarre technique of fishing for bottom-feeders is known officially as "hand fishing" because the person uses his own hand as a sort of bait.

The fisherman, or "fish tickler," usually takes off his clothes to avoid getting bogged down in the mud. Often the tickler has to be under the murky water for a couple of minutes to make sure he has a good grip on the fish. Usually a second person blocks off any other opening to the secret love nest and stands ready to pull out the tickler if the fish gets stuck in a log with an arm in its maw. The mouth of a flathead catfish is so large that supposedly a cantaloupe can fit inside.

"You stick your arm right down there in the mud real slow, and the catfish will slowly 'swallow' your arm," an older man named Rex explained. I assumed at the time that he was pulling my leg. "You can't see a thing, but you feel the fish take your whole hand in its mouth, and then you just lift it out of the water. I'm not sure why they call it 'noodling' but probably because you noodle your hand into its mouth."

As incredible as this sounds, noodling is real, but it is fraught with danger. Fish ticklers can be surprised when their bait—an arm—is bitten by a snapping turtle or beaver. And male catfish are so aggressive that they will eat their own offspring if the little ones don't leave the nest soon enough. Just like baiting a hole, noodling is illegal in most northern states, probably because of the danger.

Some catfish can erect spines that sting with a mild venom. There are three sharp spines on the dorsal and side fins but not on their barbels, or whiskers. The spines on young catfish are so sharp that Native Americans used them as needles to work on leather. In the country of Guyana in South America, some priests dubbed catfish "the devil's offspring" because they thought the stingers caused leprosy.

If frightened while enveloping the arm, a catfish can grip its sandpaper-like teeth down and halt the tickler from pushing his arm farther into the fish. If the fisherman pulls out his arm quickly, he can lose some skin or get severely scraped. Once the arm is sufficiently inside, the fisherman jabs his hand through the gills and locks his grip with his other hand. *If* the fish isn't too heavy, he can raise it to the surface and get to shore. If a catfish fights back, it will slap its tail against the log making a bang known as "thundering."

The record catfish in Minnesota weighed 70 pounds and was caught in the St. Croix River. The world record is more than 123 pounds, from waters near Independence, Kansas. Tales of much larger fish that got away are rampant. The book *Fishing for Buffalo* tells of an elderly man in Tennessee who hooked a catfish with a ham and dragged it out of the water with a mule, and "the river went down an inch." The old man let the fish go and said, "A man ain't got no right to kill somethin' as big and brave as that thar catfish."

A. George Morris, in *Sport Fishing USA*, told of another granddaddy catfish that was too smart to take any bait on a hook. A fisherman made a hook with a barb on it, tied the hook to his wrist, went down to the river, and dived in. He paddled to the hole where the catfish was and, after rubbing it on its back to quiet it down, he jerked the hook up under the catfish's jaw. "Some two weeks later, they found the man and the fish bound together about a mile down the stream, both dead. The fish had more strength than he had and held him under the water until he drowned, then finally the catfish died from pulling him down the stream. That is noodling."

To honor these giant fish lurking in the deep, the city of Wahpeton, North Dakota, on the Red River of the North, raised a forty-foot-long statue of a catfish. During the historic flood of this north-flowing river in 1997, the entire town seemed doomed as snow melted in the south but could not flow north because of ice blockage. Downstream, Grand Forks flooded and burned, and Fargo had knee-deep water running through the streets. The waters in Wahpeton crested just at the edge of the mudcat statue. Wahpper had scared off the rising tide, so the town now calls itself the "Catfish Capital of the North." A few whiskers of the "The World's Largest Catfish" are missing, likely good-luck talismans taken by hopeful anglers who fish in the old-fashioned way and don't dare noodle for any of these giant beasts of the deep.

Fishing with Flies

Impure Purists

"If fishing is a religion, fly-fishing is high church," according to former NBC news anchor Tom Brokaw. Many anglers both admire and scoff at the purity of fly-fishing. Perhaps the most famous novella and film on the sport comes from Norman Maclean, *A River Runs through It*. This bucolic story equates

Fishing with a fly requires more than just casting off the dock into the lake. The Weber Lifelike Fly Company of Stevens Point, Wisconsin, used photo comics, or "moviegrams," to give step-by-step lessons to fish like a pro. COLLECTION OF DONALD HARRISON.

Fly-fishing is the most revered way to catch fish, at least according to fly fishers. This sport requires skill, patience, endurance, arcane paraphernalia, and a great set of hand-tied flies made with exotic feathers or fur. PHOTOGRAPHS BY THE AUTHOR.

fly-fishing to philosophy with such quotations as "To him, all good things—trout as well as eternal salvation—came by grace; and grace comes by art; and art does not come easy." Maclean talks about the virtuousness of fly-fishing that is synonymous with nature: the farther one goes from these serene rivers, the closer one gets to the dark side. He wrote: "The world is full of bastards, the number increasing rapidly the further one gets from Missoula, Montana."

Author and avid fisherman Jim Harrison disparaged careless sportsmen in his essay "A Sporting Life." "Fishing becomes the mechanics of acquiring fish, bird hunting a process of 'bagging the limit,'" he wrote. "Most sportsmen have become mad Germans with closets full of arcane death equipment. To some, an ultimate sport would be chasing coyote with a 650cc snowmobile armed with an M-16."

WORTH *fishing tackle*

FLY TYING KIT
make dry flies • wet flies • streamers

Complete With:

VISE
THREAD
HACKLE
QUILLS
TINSEL
HOOKS
YARN
FLOSS
WAX
INSTRUCTIONS

FOR THE HOBBIEST WHO ENJOYS FISHING

Even the president of the United States, Herbert Hoover, weighed in on the argument of different kinds of anglers:

Although all men are equal before fish, there are some class distinctions among them. The dry-fly devotees hold themselves a bit superior to the wet-fly fishermen; the wet-fly fishermen, superior to the spinner fishermen; and the spinners, superior to the bait fishermen. I have noticed, however, that toward the end of the day when there are no strikes, each social level collapses in turn down the scale until it gets some fish for dinner.

Australian art historian Robert Hughes looks at the sport in terms of social hierarchy: "That fixed belief in the superiority of fly fishing for trout over all other ways of angling . . . where did it come from? Evidently, class. It hardly existed before the English, in the nineteenth century, turned it into a mystique." In fact an early reference to fly-fishing comes from the British book *The Compleat Angler* from 1653 that likens the sport to an art of the highest caliber: "O Sir, doubt not but that Angling is an art; is it not an art to deceive a Trout with an artificial Fly? a Trout! That is more sharp-sighted than any Hawk you have named."

What is the best way to convince these clever fish into chomping on the hook? Fisherman Geoff Johnson fished for steelhead trout, returning to the streams from Lake Superior, with a salmon-egg spawn sack. Fisherman Harmon Henkin in *Silent Seasons* broke down trout bait into "the two general types: the maggot-and-fly combinations and the insect-larvae favorites."

The idea of using bait to catch trout is nothing short of a sin to many fly-fishing traditionalists. Robert Hughes's father severely scolded him for using live bait. "You got that trout with a hopper. You will never do that again. People who use live bait on trout are not fit to fish. They are thugs. They are barbarians. They might as well be using dynamite." His father then used a "slashing stroke of the belt to my backside" and made him release the fish. His father told him, "Assume that any gun you touch is loaded. Never point it at anything you don't intend to shoot at. Never shoot anything alive unless you mean to eat it. And never, under any circumstances, fish for trout with anything but a fly."

Fisherman William Hjortsberg mocked the idea of the pure angler who must use only certain lures or bait in *Silent Seasons*, "A fisherman will sum up a companion's refusal of his offered jar of neon-orange-dyed salmon eggs in favor of a homemade concoction consisting of beef suet and lemon peel soaked in sardine oil: 'Never mind Charlie, he's a *purist*.' A purist is the 'effete snob' of the fishing fraternity." All this is a matter of opinion, obviously, but any angler will have opinions on the best bait and lures.

Even those who mock the fishers who wade into freezing waters in remote rivers respect their dedication and hardiness. As Cervantes, the author of *Don Quixote*, wrote, "There's no taking trout with dry breeches."

Besides the required physical endurance, fly-fishing enthusiasts carry on a remarkable tradition of tying flies. The oldest surviving reference to fly-fishing is by Aelian in *De Natura Animalium* (On the nature of animals) from the second century

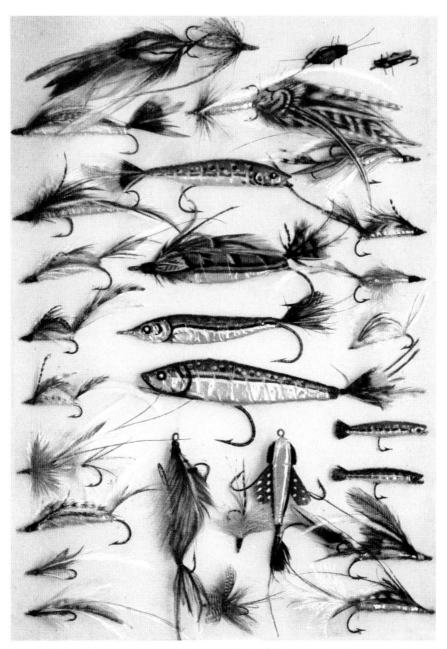

Colorful flies and lures often graced the pages of early fishing manuals. This painted illustration is from Louis Rhead, *Fisherman's Lures and Game-Fish Food* (New York: Scribner's, 1920).

AD, who described Macedonians fishing on a river near Thessaloniki who created a bee-like insect by "wrap[ping] the hook in scarlet wool, and to the wool they attach two feathers that grow beneath a cock's wattles and are the color of wax." The earliest fishing book in the English language, *Treatisse on Fyshynge* from the 1300s, written by Dame Juliana Berners in England, recommends, "In the begynning of Maye a good flye, the body of roddyd wull and lappid abowte wyth blacke silk; the wynges of the drake of the redde capons hakyll."

For millennia, fly fishers have employed all sorts of ruses to trick the trout with fur and feathers on hooks. This obsession with finding the most unusual materials led some purists astray. Environmentalist Ted Williams exposed in his book *Something Fishy* that the law enforcement division of the U.S. Fish and Wildlife Service went undercover to discover "more than a dozen prominent fly shops . . . at least six knowingly dealing in black-market materials for classic salmon flies." Williams wrote that two agents went incognito and reported, "We had an individual who was smuggling in large volumes of polar bear hair and bragging about how he could get all these junglefowl capes in from Canada." One of the dealers, who asked to remain anonymous, told Williams, "Lately there's this cult—this whole thing of ownership of rare materials. You go to any antique show or sportsmen's show, it's like a nightclub. You whisper and you can get the stuff, just like you can get cocaine. Chatterer, Indian crow, toucan, macaw . . . There's a lot of muffled talk, deals going down all the time." Williams takes on the idea of what makes for a pure fishing experience and what is just posing: "We posture ourselves as righteous sportsmen and go into fits if we see a spin fisherman squeeze a six-inch brook trout. But we can put the kill order on birds in Venezuela." If fly-fishing is indeed so spiritually sublime, wouldn't this be heresy?

'Gators! 'Gators!
Invasive Creatures of the Deep

I was wandering by the Mississippi River in St. Paul with my camera around my neck when a woman swerved her giant Ford Escape. She rolled down her window and frantically asked, "Are you here about the alligator?"

I nervously asked if an alligator was on the loose. She had thought I was the reporter she was expecting, who arrived a few minutes later. A television news crew pulled up in a van with a large antenna projecting from the roof. A slick news anchor hopped out of the van and worked on his hair in a mirror and tried to keep the thick layer of foundation on his face from cracking. As the woman spoke excitedly with the TV crew, I spoke with a man on the banks of the river. He showed me snapshots he had taken of the alligator in the water. "My guess is that it's only a couple of feet long. On the TV news, though, they'll make him look huge," he said. "There he is!" I noticed what looked like a small log floating on the water. The alligator went underwater as we approached. "It's not the alligators that you have to worry about so much as the carp. They'll eat anything," he said, but I was still worried.

When the TV crew arrived at the water, they were

making so much noise that the alligator wouldn't come back. The woman carried an enormous net in hopes of catching the creature and getting on the evening news. Meanwhile, a policeman came down to the shore to see what the commotion was about. I explained that we saw an alligator in the river, but he wasn't too impressed. "This is nothing," he replied. "We've seen much weirder stuff than this in the river." I asked him to elaborate, but he replied cryptically, "You don't wanna know."

Apparently, all sorts of strange creatures appear in northern lakes and rivers that don't belong there. In the summer of 2012, newspapers reported that a "testicle-eating fish" with humanlike teeth, a close relative of the piranha, had been seen in Lake Lou Yaeger in Litchfield, Illinois, outside of Chicago. The pacu is generally vegetarian, but some claim it is omnivorous, and it is native to South American freshwater rivers, especially the Amazon. Down there, the fish can reach up to fifty-five pounds, but here they can't survive a northern winter. Stacey Leasca at *MinnPost* reported in 2012, "The pacu is lovingly referred to as the 'ball cutter' after killing two men in Papua New Guinea by biting off [their] testicles." The pacu in the United States are likely pet fish released into the wild by owners who couldn't take care of them and didn't want to see them die. A second pacu was caught, this time in Lake Erie; it weighed two pounds and measured fourteen inches long. The couple who caught the fish put it on ice and later ate it.

Alligators lollygagging in lakes mostly result in calls to the police. In 2010, Wisconsin conservation coordinator Tom Zagar heard a report that an

With its strange, human-like teeth, the native South American pacu was dubbed the "ball cutter" after reports circulated that the fish chomped on male swimmers' unmentionables.
PHOTOGRAPH BY HENRIK CARL, NATURAL HISTORY MUSEUM OF DENMARK.

alligator was sunning on the mudflats of Lake Muskego. Alligators usually elude capture, but Zagar told Newsradio 620, "We cast a lure at it. It actually became hooked and we were able to unhook it, and it's doing fine now." He tried to assure nervous residents that it would "eat frogs and small fish and things like that. It probably was happy for a while, but Wisconsin has a cruel winter."

This is a common theme when trying to calm

people who are worried they may get munched on while swimming. Wisconsin warden Mike Clutter said, "It would not have survived the winter out there" when the *Milwaukee Sentinel* reported on July 20, 2014, that a four-foot alligator was captured in the Sheboygan River. "The gator's snout was taped shut for the officers' safety," and the police put the giant lizard into a dog cage. The beast was sent to a reptile rescue operation in Illinois.

Also in 2014, Helen Zumbaum heard unusual sounds in the long grass on the pond behind her house in Nowthen, Minnesota. She noticed a three- to four-foot alligator just twenty feet away. The *St. Paul Pioneer Press* reported, "At least three alligators were spotted last year in Washington County." Zumbaum told a reporter from that newspaper, "At first I thought it was a rag or something else kind of bumpy, but then I looked again and it was like, 'OK, this is for real.'" The Minnesota Department of Natural Resources dubbed it an invasive species, so a police officer shot the animal twice after they couldn't capture it.

This is common procedure for errant alligators. In Scandia, Minnesota, in August 2013, the head of the parks and trails division warned residents along the lake that two alligators measuring about forty inches in length were on the loose in Goose Lake. Residents were jumpy after a five-foot boa constrictor had been found at a home not far away in Stillwater. The DNR shot one of the alligators, but Sarah Richard of the Minnesota Herpetological Society complained that shooting was too much. "You're talking about a two-foot alligator who couldn't hurt anybody. To go out and shoot it . . . it's unnecessary," she told the *Pioneer*

Press. Her organization adopts between two hundred to three hundred reptiles each year, and about one-fourth of those were strays who were probably released into the wild by pet owners.

Alternative Fishing Techniques
Dynamiting for Dinner

When early Europeans arrived in the Midwest, they noted how Native Americans caught their fish. In 1669, Jesuit missionaries traveled through New France and wrote in *Travels and Explorations* that the Ojibwe used nets made of willow bark or wild hemp and weighted the mesh with stones. They speared fish with sharp tips made from chiseled stone or bone, which made great hooks. The book described another method, a cross between spearing and netting: "Dexterity and strength are needed for this kind of fishing; for one must stand upright in a bark canoe, and there, among the whirlpools, with muscles tense, thrust deep into the water a rod, at the end of which is fastened a net made in the form of a pocket into which the fish are made to enter . . . six or seven large fish being taken each time."

One of the fish they went after was the gar. Along with sturgeon, these are ancient fish essentially dating back to the Cretaceous period during the time of the dinosaurs. These prehistoric-looking creatures breathe air from the surface by turning on their sides like a swimmer, so they are able to live in stagnant water. "The gar's armorlike scales and ability to breathe air helped it outsurvive dinosaurs, woolly mammoths, and prehistoric peoples," accord-

In 1669, Jesuit missionaries described the Ojibwe spearing fish in what was then New France: "Dexterity and strength are needed for this kind of fishing," as well as patience and good aim.
PHOTOGRAPH BY ROLAND W. REED, CIRCA 1925. COURTESY OF THE MINNESOTA HISTORICAL SOCIETY.

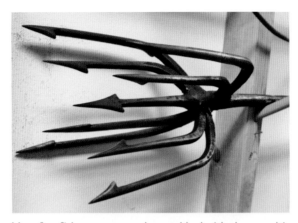

Very few fish can escape when stabbed with these multi-pronged weapons, especially with barbs to prevent a quick getaway. PHOTOGRAPH BY THE AUTHOR.

ing to *Fishing for Buffalo*. These early tribes, "working across North America from Asia, used clubs and spears to capture the fish. . . . At night they cruised the shallows in canoes or dugouts, with torches ablaze on long poles overhead, and speared gar illuminated below."

When the Native Americans were forced to give up their land, fishing rights were usually preserved in the treaties but often not recognized by the authorities. An editorial in the *Hennepin County Mirror* from Minneapolis on April 8, 1880, decried this injustice, saying, "Natives can't spear a fish—'tis against the law," while white fisherman can catch so many that they just throw them out, "but no spearing is allowed in the winter. This is called justice." The European settlers adopted many of the Natives Americans' fishing techniques. On September 11, 1852, the *Weekly Minnesotian* reported that Simon Stevens built the first recorded icehouse on Lake Minnetonka in which

he built a small fire and cut a good-sized hole in the ice. The fish came to investigate, and he speared fish as fast as a neighbor could sell them.

A. George Morris in *Sport Fishing USA* describes spearing with a gig, a multipronged spear similar to Poseidon's trident. "First you have to obtain a gig, not any old gig that you can buy at the store, but one fashioned from the steel of a wood rasp. . . . Stand on the end of a johnboat and go down a stream laced with rapids. . . . By the light of a gasoline lantern, [when you] spot a fish out in the stream, throw the gig for twenty-five feet in five feet of water, and hit a fish running for its life." If you snag a gar, you'll be in for the fight of your life—they are known to be one of the most vicious of fighting fish and very hard to land. If a gar bites on an old-fashioned hook, guidebooks recommend cutting the line. The stomach acids of the fish will likely dissolve the metal hook within a month.

"About the gar the less said the better; some shoot arrows at them, others prefer dynamite," wrote fisherman William Hjortsberg in *Silent Seasons*. Although highly illegal now, catching dinner with dynamite, or "blast fishing," was the lazy man's version of angling. Some fish floated to the surface to be snatched up after the blast, but many of the fish died and sank to the bottom to rot. For many fishers, reels and fancy rods were only for the elite. *St. Paul Pioneer Press* writer Chris Niskanen wrote on April 26, 1999: "Anglers kept virtually every fish they caught. Putting food on the table was a primary goal of *fishing*." Because of this, dynamite was not uncommon as a favorite fishing technique.

Niskanen describes another special resource

called "fish berries," a small fruit from India. The fish gobbled up the toxic berries and turned belly up, then hungry fishers just scooped dinner into the boat. The only problem was that these berries were toxic to humans as well, and the resulting violent indigestion forced fishers to abandon the berries.

Another questionable approach to catching fish still happens in some European fishing competitions. Contestants will attract the fish to their plot ahead of time by lobbing balls of maggots into the river with a slingshot. This idea of feeding fish at a particular spot and returning later to snag them is generally illegal in the north woods, but some anglers stock up on "trout feed," usually intended for fish farms, to convince finicky fish that this is the place to get the good stuff. *Sport Fishing USA* even recommends underwater music to soothe and attract curious fish. "Try hanging the ear phone to the radio down underwater to attract fish to your location. It will work! . . . A curious bluegill took a nip at my ear phone and almost got away with radio and all. It might be well to equip your ear phone with a hook, just in case a 5-pound bass decides that the mechanism is a new kind of bug!"

The book also recommends "jug fishing," a sport perfect for those who don't want to waste their day waiting for a nibble. Tie a length of fishing line to empty, sealed bleach bottles or other buoys. Attach a sinker and hook to the end of the line with whatever bait is best. "If you are able to swipe a pair of your wife's hose—or you can always talk her out of a pair with runs in them—you are in business," *Sport Fishing USA* recommended. "Cut a nylon stocking in small squares, insert any ingredient that you think a fish will bite, and tie it into a ball. Put this on your hook."

Then sit back and see if the jugs bob up and down with a hungry fish on the other end. While jug fishing is generally illegal in the north, some states add the supposedly draconian rule that the jugs must be checked every twenty-four hours. "This kind of fishing is similar to getting money from home without writing for it."

If this is too much bother and no dynamite is handy, just grab a baseball bat and head to the creek. The *St. Paul Daily Globe* described this improbable practice, reporting on July 3, 1890, how impatient fishers strode into the river to bonk two- to four-pound carp on the head. "The peculiar part of the sport, however, is that a hook and line are not necessary. The fishers roll up their trousers and wade in. Armed with a club, they strike the fish over the head, and when he keels over they pick him out."

Walking on Water

The Dangers of Ice Fishing

In the frozen north, devout anglers walk on water. Southerners won't believe that we drive pickups to little houses on top of frozen water just to fish through a hole. How do we stay warm? A heater keeps it toasty despite the floor of ice.

On major ice fishing lakes, broad roads are plowed nearly one hundred feet wide with stop signs warning of a junction with a crossing ice path, even though nothing will block the view except for maybe a mountain of plowed snow. Early one morning on Lake Mille Lacs in central Minnesota, I saw a pickup stuck on a mound after the driver tried to jump a

Properly made spears were strong enough to nab even the most finicky fish from the rapids. Photographer H. H. Bennett captured this image of a man spearing a sturgeon at a dam near Kilbourn, Wisconsin (later Wisconsin Dells). COURTESY OF THE WISCONSIN HISTORICAL SOCIETY, WHI-7287.

LAKE MINNETONKA.

No. 2695

These dapper gentlemen seem to think that bopping a fish on the head is the only way to ensure a successful catch. COURTESY OF THE WESTONKA HISTORICAL SOCIETY.

four-foot snowbank. Three other pickups pushed and pulled the embedded truck, while the driver held his head, ashamed that his four-wheel drive hadn't set him free. He had abandoned his truck the night before when the wheels kept spinning; he had stumbled back to his shack in the dark. Now they were racing against time to free the vehicle before the ice melted in the spring.

For the most part, there is no speed limit on frozen lakes, leading to occasional ice races or fearless drivers surpassing sixty miles per hour on these slippery roads. "That's not very smart, because you can hit a piece of ice and have a blowout," Mille Lacs resort owner Frank Dressely told the *New York Times* on January 27, 1992. Early in the fall and late in the spring, some risk dubious ice and ignore warnings. Inevitably, a few pickups and snowmobiles find a watery grave at the bottom of the lake. Walleye bite at the beginning of the season, so die-hard fishermen can't wait to get their houses out on the ice and risk everything for a nibble. Each year cars and icehouses crack the thin ice. "Keep your window rolled down a little so you can open the door if we go through," fisherman Brad Hanson told me as he drove his two-ton Jeep over Lake Mille Lacs to an icehouse.

Occasionally deep, unexpected crevasses form and icebergs break off and float into open water. At the end of December 2011 on a lake near Brainerd, Minnesota, ice under several ice shanties and ATVs broke off and drifted away. "One man felt like he was trolling," Brainerd fire chief Kevin Stunek told the

Minneapolis Star Tribune on December 29, 2011. "He stepped out of his fishing house and saw he was on the move." The ice was seven to ten inches thick, enough to hold the icehouse, but the nervous anglers floated a good five hundred feet away from the rest of the ice. The sheriff's department pulled out hovercrafts and canoes to rescue the fishers, who had to leave their houses and vehicles until the water froze again and connected the iceberg to the mainland.

Anglers were enticed to put all sorts of snake oil remedies on their bait or lures to catch that hungry walleye. Notice the warning not to judge Doodle Oil "on one day's performance" but give it credit when the fish actually are biting, which begs the question, what good does it do? PHOTOGRAPHS BY THE AUTHOR.

This is one way to catch a fish. Outside New Ulm, Minnesota, along the Cottonwood River circa 1890, the laws didn't forbid such explosive techniques for putting supper on the table. COURTESY OF THE MINNESOTA HISTORICAL SOCIETY.

A lonely icehouse on Lake Mille Lacs in central Minnesota is connected with plowed roads, many with stop signs. Pizza delivery and other services often reach the icy colonies of anglers. PHOTOGRAPH BY THE AUTHOR.

Ice tsunamis are another northern phenomenon that can strike when a patch of open water forms. These have nothing to do with underwater earthquakes. In May 2013 along Lake Mille Lacs in central Minnesota, forty-mile-per-hour winds rammed giant sheets of ice into the shore and against buildings along the banks to form thirty-foot-high hills of ice.

The biggest danger is breaking through thin ice and freezing to death. Minnesota fisherman Geoff Johnson told me that this risk is far overblown: "It's not really such a big deal to fall through the ice." To get to the best, most remote ice fishing holes, he and friends ski into the Boundary Waters Canoe Area

Wilderness, where no motorized vehicles are allowed. Sometimes the ice is too thin: "The lake trout fishing in the Boundary Waters is great in the spring when the ice can be rotten and dangerous. The worst is falling through with cross-country skis because they keep catching on the ice when you try to pull yourself out. Or if there's moving water where you break through, which there usually is, the current catches

Springtime
WARNING
To Ice Fishermen

your skis and kind of pulls you under." He told me about a dangerous trip on Lake Mille Lacs when six of them were on four snowmobiles that went into the water. He shrugged it off. "Climbing out isn't as difficult as everyone makes it out to be. I carry picks, but you can use your keys as a pick to pull yourself out or let your sleeves freeze to the surface and then climb out." Their snowmobiles, on the other hand, went straight to the bottom.

Rumors run rampant about cold, lonely ice fishermen in search of companionship to warm them up. Gossip about icehouse hookers knocking on the door is perhaps akin to stories about mermaids leading poor sailors astray. The *Philadelphia Inquirer* on February 3, 2003, summed up the salacious speculation: "No one ever proved it, but few ever really

Foolhardy fishermen refuse to believe that the ice is too thin. An old junked jalopy, stuck on the ice and slowly sinking to the bottom of the lake, is a sure sign of spring. COLLECTION OF DONALD HARRISON.

The 1948 St. Paul Winter Carnival included an ice fishing competition that brought generations of Minnesotans together, in spite of freezing temperatures. PHOTOGRAPH BY *MINNEAPOLIS STAR AND TRIBUNE.* COURTESY OF THE MINNESOTA HISTORICAL SOCIETY.

doubted it." To find out for myself, I called the sheriffs of Aitkin and Mille Lacs Counties, who split jurisdiction on the most popular ice fishing lake in Minnesota, Mille Lacs. Both departments chose not to speak on the record, which, of course, furthers speculation by imaginative ice fishermen with too much time on their hands. The bartender at one resort that rents icehouses would neither confirm nor deny any reports, but he did point out that nearly all his icehouses were rented. "No one is catching a goddamn thing! Ever heard of fishing widows?"

The most common actual crime might be multiple lines in the water. Conservation officer Curt Rossow wrote in *Some Just Get Away* that he caught a fisherman with four lines down (the maximum allowed is two at a time). "When he found out which holes the fish were biting the best in, he was going to use only two lines!" The culprit took the ticket and threw it on the ice—and picked it up when the officer threatened a littering ticket, too. He later wrote to the judge saying that he should be pardoned because he donates all the fish to the senior home in town. "He also stated that if President Ford could pardon President Nixon, surely the judge could pardon him!" The fishing offender was not pardoned.

Another multiple-line perpetrator fought the ticket in court by claiming he didn't have a lure or bait on the other line, just a beer attached to it to keep it cold. After that incident, Rossow always double-checked to make sure each of the lines was baited. He nabbed another violator with four lines in the holes, but the fisherman explained that his wife had just stepped out and was coming back. He got a ticket. The officer found his wife in the next ice shack,

also with four lines down. "She told us that her husband had just left and would be back soon," Rossow wrote. She was ticketed as well.

The idea that ice fishing is somehow a deviant sport gained steam when the *International Herald Tribune* ran an article on February 25, 2013, called "Keeping Ice Fishing Free from Doping." Since ice fishermen were pushing for this frozen pastime to be an Olympic sport, the U.S. Anti-Doping Agency descended on the World Ice Fishing Championship at the Plaza Hotel in Wausau, Wisconsin, and made contestants provide a urine sample to prove they were clean. "We do not test for beer, because then everybody would fail," said Joel McDearmon, chairman of the U.S. Freshwater Fishing Federation. No signs of doping were found.

Competitive ice fishing seems to be clean, but the recreational sport is used by some deviants as a front for illicit activities. The Associated Press reported on January 29, 1999, that three young men manufactured methamphetamine in an ice house on Waverly Lake thirty miles west of Minneapolis; one officer who entered the shack had to be hospitalized from the fumes. On August 30, 2002, the Minnesota State Supreme Court upheld a decision that the police need permission before entering an icehouse; obtaining a search warrant for obviously illegal activities can occur quickly but still gives offenders a chance to hide any evidence. The *New York Post* reported on February 13, 2005, that meth laboratories on North Dakota lakes are hard to bust. North Dakota attorney general Wayne Stenehjem said, "It's a double hazard. As soon as [authorities] come up on one of the ice houses, evidence is dumped down the hole and those

What to do with free time between bites? Deal the cards and light a cigar. These fishermen are in a state-of-the-art ice shanty circa 1953 and have already caught their daily limit. PHOTOGRAPH BY *MINNEAPOLIS STAR JOURNAL TRIBUNE*. COURTESY OF THE MINNESOTA HISTORICAL SOCIETY.

Clever heaters like the Heat-Pal from Sweden and the Seater Heater kept an angler's tush toasty on frigid days. But sitting on this heated metal pan could give the feeling of being cooked for dinner. PHOTOGRAPHS BY THE AUTHOR.

toxic chemicals go into the lake," which is terrible for the health of the fish and anyone who eats them. The *Fergus Falls Daily Journal* reported a similar case on October 29, 2010, when a Minnesota DNR conservation officer was checking fishing licenses at icehouses. He caught two young men on Eagle Lake trying to hide syringes, spoons, and other meth paraphernalia. Assured Decontamination Services in Minneapolis cleaned up the mess armed with hazmat suits and breathing masks. A representative told me, "We try to get all of the chemicals before they can sink down into the lake. Fortunately meth labs in icehouses are few and far between."

You would think that the biggest danger around

ice fishing is tedium, but as Jim Harrison wrote in *Silent Seasons*, "The true force behind ice fishing is that it is better than no fishing at all." Being in a shack with subzero winds whistling outside and no fish biting leads to odd pastimes. I've witnessed my share of card games, stupid science tricks like freezing soap bubbles, bets on whether full beer bottles float (they don't) and how long someone can stand outside in underwear (thirty seconds). All this was disturbed by a knock on the icehouse door. It wasn't the police, but a well-oiled man who had abandoned his pickup for the moment and asked if this is where the party is. He walked on the water to move on to the next shack.

Ice Castles

Fishing in "Luxury"

"I have friends who essentially live in their icehouses during the winter," Minnesota fisherman Geoff Johnson told me. "One of them was going through a divorce, so he put his fish house on Carson's Bay with bunks, a propane stove, and a kitchenette. He set up a P.O. box for his mail and then got a membership at U.S. Swim and Fitness so he could shower before work. You don't need to be rich to live right on Lake Minnetonka—in fact, you can be destitute. He caught tons of fish that year; probably the best year of his life!"

Although I'm not convinced this bachelor pad on ice was exactly smart, it certainly was creative. I've been in fishing cabins set on stilts on the famous cod fishing islands of Lofoten in northern Norway, where crafty fishermen had drilled holes in the floorboards so they could sit to fish when the tide came in under the building. I needed to see how some clever bachelors lived in the winter on the frozen lakes, so a couple of fishermen friends brought me to one of the most famous wallcye lakes in Minnesota, Mille Lacs. The *New York Times* reported that about five thousand shanties are set up each winter on the lake with up to twenty-five thousand people sleeping on the ice—considerably more than any of the towns on the shore.

The ultimate luxury in ice fishing hails from Montevideo, Minnesota. Solar panels, a mini bathroom, a full kitchen, and comfy beds—just make sure the ice is thick enough! PHOTOGRAPHS BY KAREN BOGAN. COURTESY OF ICE CASTLE FISH HOUSES.

We went to a year-round resort that had a bar crammed with snowmobilers and tables full of beer glasses. The bartender doubled as the registration clerk and assigned the fishing shanties. "Just drive out a mile or so on the lake and turn left. You're number 26," he told us. The price was higher than a cheap motel that would at least have provided sheets and blankets and no mysterious garbage pile in the corner. Obviously this wasn't a luxury fish house.

The pilot light in the big rusty can heater had blown out before we opened the door, so a thick smell of gas greeted us. We kept the door open, jammed a flaming piece of cardboard into the heater, and it roared to life. I didn't mind my singed eyebrows because the warmth was worth it. Just as dramatically as the stove had heated, it extinguished itself, and gas leaked into the room as the temperature dropped. My friends explained the dilemma: a well-insulated ice shanty that doesn't let in fresh air can be dangerous because we could be asphyxiated from the carbon monoxide of a bad stove, but leaky walls could cause us to freeze to death.

We drove back to the bar and confronted the caretaker of the ice shacks who questioned whether we were really afraid of that "little ol' heater." When I suggested that we might never wake up again if we slept in there, he shrugged off my concern as if I were pure wimp. "I'd crank the damn thing up as hot as it goes. If you get cold, just wake up and light the sucker up again!" Finally acknowledging that we wanted to get up the next morning, he said, "I don't know if you deserve it, but dammit! We're going to give you a real damn luxury icehouse—an eight-holer!" Obviously he didn't think we deserved this princess castle since we weren't men enough to handle a real icehouse. We asked the bartender what was wrong with the caretaker. "Oh, he's not so bad, just give him a couple of drinks and he'll calm down." I wasn't sure that was a smart idea considering how he swerved into the parking lot and that he needed to go back on the ice to start the heater in our "deluxe" shack.

The only difference between the leaky icehouse and this luxury one was four holes versus eight and a working heater. We set up lines in the water and felt our feet freeze on the icy floors. Our foreheads dripped with sweat—at ceiling height it was easily ninety-five degrees. Sleeping on the top bunk meant heatstroke, and on the lower it meant hypothermia. As I fell asleep and heard snowmobilers shouting like drunk demons outside, I remembered that the ninth circle of Dante's *Inferno* had the devil frozen in a lake.

After our night in the supposed lap of luxury, I heard about Ice Castle Fish Houses made in Montevideo, Minnesota. We would have been happy with a generator to give some light, but these fish houses on wheels have optional solar panels, electric awnings, LED lighting throughout, and a satellite dish for per-

fect television reception to watch football games while fishing. The ultimate model is the eight-by-thirty-foot "King's Castle" with a triple-axle frame and hydraulic lift. Bay windows and a skylight illuminate the cedar walls. Imagine preparing dinner in the full kitchen with refrigerator, microwave, and three-burner range and then sitting in front of the electric fireplace and watching the big-screen TV. Before slumbering in one of the two double beds, stop in the bathroom—no need to freeze outside. And there are ten fishing holes in the floor with special lighting.

Ice Castle representative Karen Bogan explained that these fancy models can run up to thirty-six thousand dollars. "People made fun of us when we put air conditioning on them," she said. "What do you need with AC on an ice house? But these double as RVs in the summer." Many have plumbing that is used primarily in the summer since the frozen lake doesn't have water and sewage hookups. Because of the plumbing in these icehouses/RVs, they can count as a summer home and might offer tax deductions.

These deluxe houses weigh between 4,800 to 7,000 pounds, but Bogan said not to worry too much about the weight. "If the ice is thick enough for the truck that pulls the fish house, it's thick enough for the Ice Castle." I wondered if any had fallen through. "Oh, yeah, they've fallen through. It's a mess when they're hauled back up. The electronics can get destroyed."

I asked if anyone lives all winter on the lake amid these amenities. "Oh, yeah. A lot of guys get laid off in the winter and then essentially live in their fish houses. How long do they stay there? I suppose it depends on how long they they can stand each other without a shower."

Boulder Junction, Wisconsin, celebrates its status as the trademarked "Musky Capital of the World" with the annual Musky Jamboree. These two brave event organizers help prepare for the fishy feast on August 9, 1972. PHOTOGRAPH BY THE WISCONSIN DEPARTMENT OF NATURAL RESOURCES. COURTESY OF THE WISCONSIN HISTORICAL SOCIETY, WHI-66609.

CHAPTER FOUR

Fish Festivals
Get Your Bullheads Here!

Fishing is boring, unless you catch an actual fish, and then it is disgusting.

—Dave Barry

Many towns relish the fame that can come from exalting the unusual culture surrounding fishing. Aitkin, Minnesota, hosts an annual Fish House Parade on Main Street with everything from milk-carton icehouses to rocket-shaped shacks. Some participants pimp up their icehouse with electric generators for television and lights and, of course, drink holders. To celebrate the ugliest fish imaginable, ice fishers gather on the middle of Leech Lake every winter to haul in slimy, prehistoric-looking eelpout in subzero weather. The residents of Waterville couldn't figure out how to rid their town lake of stinging bullheads, so they declared an annual festival to fry up as many as possible. If you can't beat 'em, eat 'em.

Just as potatoes were considered "patriotic" food, since more bread and flour could then be shipped to the front in World War I, replenishing stocks of fish was intended to feed folks on the home front, as promoted in this lithographic poster by Charles Livingston Bull from 1917. LIBRARY OF CONGRESS PRINTS AND PHOTOGRAPHS DIVISION.

day his best, which also marks the beginning of the next campaign season. It is the governor's sacred duty to inaugurate the season on opening day, and the media has a feeding frenzy at this historic event. For people who fish, this day is a chance to initiate another season and sip a six-pack on the waves.

National Fish Day

"Eat What You Wish, But Eat Some Fish"

"Eat More Fish!" trumpeted the campaign by the U.S. government during World War I. The posters argued, "Save the products of the land. Eat more fish—they feed themselves." The idea was to "SAVE the MEAT for Our Soldiers and Allies" since fish spoiled more readily and the troops needed the protein from meat. In 1921, *Pacific Fisherman* boasted, "High meat prices and the government's 'Eat More Fish' campaign during the war have revived interest in fish [as] food."

After the war the fish industry didn't want to lose momentum. The Bureau of Fisheries met in Washington, D.C., to declare a National Fish Day after seeing the success of Salmon Day in Canada. The clever Canadians wisely chose the first day of Lent to kick off their fish-eating effort, whereas the Americans set March 9 as the annual date. The lyrical advertisements waxed poetic, advising, "Eat what you wish, but eat some fish. The national fish day is in honor of the fishermen who daily risk their lives to furnish us with fish, which is a wholesome dish."

According to *Pacific Fisherman,* the Bureau of Fisheries spread the word across the country as an

Much to the chagrin of moms everywhere, the fishing opener in Minnesota falls on the same weekend as Mother's Day, leaving fishing widows throughout the state. Still, the Minnesota governor gives the excuse for politicians to have a bully pulpit to trumpet the joys of eating fish. "Arrangements have been made for National Fish Day dinners on the night of March 9 in a large number of cities where leading operators and public men will discuss fishery matters." This national campaign attempted to get notices in all newspapers, especially those with many lakes or on the coasts.

Grand Rapids, Minnesota, tried to spread the word across the northland with this notice in the *Grand Rapids Herald-Review* in 1921:

TO PUT NATIONAL FISH DAY ACROSS IN YOUR TOWN:

- Invite your leading public men to be present to speak on fisheries. . . . Arrange a National Fish Day Dinner with aid of your Chamber of Commerce. See proprietors of moving picture theatres and ask them to feature fish films in the news service.

- A fish a day is something we of Northern Minnesota should encourage for the reason that we have the fish. . . . Those big fellows down in the bottom of the lake are strong and healthy and awaiting an angler who is impatiently looking forward to the opening of the season. One cannot eat fish without thinking of exciting moments, outstanding events of a lifetime, not in importance, but in pleasure.

To eat roast beef does not stir one's sporting blood. A leg o' lamb doesn't excite one's imagination. But taste of good fish—it is a better spring tonic than dandelion wine.

Fish was considered hardship food by those who liked a meat-and-potatoes supper, so the U.S. Office of War released this propaganda poster during the height of World War II to encourage people to eat fish at home. OFFICE OF WAR INFORMATION, 1943. HENRY KOERNER, ARTIST. WORLD WAR II POSTER COLLECTION AT NORTHWESTERN UNIVERSITY LIBRARY.

There's plenty of smelt for everyone as fishers haul up hundreds of smelt running in Menominee, Michigan. COURTESY OF JACK DEO, SUPERIOR VIEW PHOTOGRAPHY.

National Fish Day made a big splash only in 1921. Despite national efforts, the tradition didn't take, perhaps because Friday was already established in many people's minds as the day for fish fries.

Smelt Wrestling

"Run, Smelt, Run!"

In the early 1900s, fisheries introduced smelt into tributary rivers of Lake Michigan in an attempt to feed the newly seeded Atlantic salmon (lake trout) in the Great Lakes. Most efforts failed, but by 1923 Lake Michigan had a thriving smelt population, and the little fish found their way into all the Great Lakes by 1930.

Then the problems began. Invasive sea lamprey killed off the lake trout by sucking out their guts. Smelt flourished because of the lack of predators and even ate the fingerlings of their biggest competitors, cisco (lake herring). Soon, in the spring, massive smelt runs clogged the rivers around Lake Michigan.

In 1931 less than one hundred thousand pounds of smelt were caught commercially in Lake Michigan, but a decade later the number rose to nearly five million pounds. So many smelt would run that beaches along the Great Lakes in the 1940s were cleaned with bulldozers to clear the dead smelt that couldn't find enough food.

The Menominee River between the twin cities of Marinette, Wisconsin, and Menominee, Michigan, became a major source of smelt in the late 1930s. One million pounds of smelt were harvested annually here. The Twin City Smelt Festival ran between 1936 and 1941, with bonfires and smelt feeds on the waterfront. Residents crowned an annual "smelt queen," who must have had a good sense of humor. "God Bless America" was belted out by Carl Zeidler, Milwaukee's "singing mayor" who had just defeated the town's six-term socialist mayor and would soon be followed by another socialist, Carl's brother Frank. This colossal quantity of fresh fish could never be consumed by locals, so organizers filled a wrestling ring with fingerlings and two brave wrestlers tussled knee-deep in the slimy smelt. Spectators gasped but couldn't resist snapping photographs. The festival ended abruptly in 1942 when most of the smelt inexplicably died off, probably from disease.

Commercial fishing of smelt in Lake Superior began in the 1950s when the population boomed again. Into the 1970s, commercial fishermen netted one to two million pounds each year. The "mythic" smelt run in 1976 produced four million pounds

What better way to celebrate smelt than to crown a king of Smeltiana? COURTESY OF JACK DEO, SUPERIOR VIEW PHOTOGRAPHY.

Fill a ring with smelt, strip down to shorts, then wrestle in the slimy mess. Marinette, Wisconsin, hosted the annual Smelt Carnival in 1939 and 1940 with a smelt wrestling event that delighted spectators—who kept their distance lest they be hit by an errant fish. PHOTOGRAPH BY THE WISCONSIN CONSERVATION DEPARTMENT. COURTESY OF THE WISCONSIN HISTORICAL SOCIETY, WHI-1969.

of smelt from Lake Superior alone. Dan Falbo was a student at the University of Minnesota Duluth during one of the runs. "It would be a drunken party of people wading in the Lester River," he told me. "When someone felt the fish swimming by their legs they'd yell, 'The smelt are running!' and everyone would jump in with buckets and scoop out as many as they wanted. We'd bring them back to the dorms and clean them in the sinks, at least until the university put up signs to not clean fish in the bathrooms."

Now, with the sea lamprey controlled, the trout population has returned to keep the smelt population in check. The smelt still run in the spring, but not as they once did. To keep the spirit, the Magic Smelt

When word spread that the smelt were running, hungry fishers gathered buckets, nets, or anything else they could find to scoop up the little fingerlings. COURTESY OF JACK DEO, SUPERIOR VIEW PHOTOGRAPHY.

Demonstrating his pride in Minnesota's outdoor offerings, Governor Wendell Anderson—with northern pike in hand—made a memorable appearance on the cover of *Time* magazine in August 1973.

Puppet Troupe of Duluth sponsors the annual Run, Smelt, Run! parade at the end of April every year since 2012. Human puppets dressed as Neptune and Old Man Winter lead the procession from Canal Park to the Zeitgeist Arts Center in Duluth for a big smelt fry at Teatro Zuccone. The organizers have revived Marinette and Menominee's tradition of crowning a "smelt queen," who has her honor guard decked out with fleur-de-lis painted on their miter hats. Let's see if anyone is brave enough to revive smelt wrestling.

The Governor's Fishing Opener

Presidents and Politicians Act the Part

Politicians are always desperate to appear as one of the people, and nothing achieves this better than fishing. President Herbert Hoover often made fun of other presidents who wanted to take up his favorite pastime. "No political aspirant can qualify for election unless he demonstrates he is a fisherman, there being twenty-five million persons who pay annually for a license to fish," he wrote in *Fishing for Fun*. "All men are equal before fish. . . . Fishing reduces the ego in Presidents and former Presidents, for at fishing most men are not equal to boys." Either that or they try to show how heroic they are.

The Minnesota governor always wets a line for the fishing opener. Governor Luther Youngdahl was in search of the spotlight in 1950 to inaugurate the "World's Largest Tiger Muskie" statue in Nevis and cracked jokes about Swedes and fish tales. The thirty-foot fish he dedicated has ribs of wood and scales of concrete with a wide-open mouth so passing tourists

In 1907, *Puck* magazine illustrator Louis Glackens spoofed a rotund presidential candidate, William Howard Taft, as he fished for the Republican nomination. The original caption read "I've got a permit." LIBRARY OF CONGRESS PRINTS AND PHOTOGRAPHS DIVISION.

can snap a photograph with their arms being gobbled up by the fish. Fishing is bipartisan, so politicians make sure they are available for the opener or at least make an appearance at festivals such as Nevis's Muskie Days in July.

Many U.S. presidents were avid, competent fishermen, such as George Washington, Thomas Jefferson, Herbert Hoover, Chester Arthur, Grover Cleveland, Dwight Eisenhower, and Jimmy Carter. Others weren't quite as proficient but felt they needed to try the sport to get elected. William McKinley, Woodrow Wilson, and Warren Harding all took up fishing. After World War II, General Dwight Eisenhower was photographed with three fish—and soon became president. President Grover Cleveland took the intellectual road by philosophizing: "It is impossible to avoid the conclusion that the fishing habit . . . tends

Before ascending to the presidency, General Dwight D. Eisenhower proudly displayed this muskie, which he caught on Pine Lake in Iron County, Wisconsin, on July 17, 1946. Harley McKeague manned the oars while Ike's younger brother Milton looked on.
PHOTOGRAPH BY STABER W. REESE. COURTESY OF THE WISCONSIN DEPARTMENT OF NATURAL RESOURCES.

directly to the increase of the intellectual power of its votaries and through them to the improvement of our national character." Most fishers yawned.

Herbert Hoover poked fun at these amateurs acting as sportsmen just to get votes. He mocked President Calvin Coolidge when he fished for trout with worms and "ten million fly fishermen at once evidenced disturbed minds." Coolidge then took up fly-fishing and the Secret Service ducked for cover. Hoover teased Senator William Howard Taft when he was photographed awkwardly clutching a fish "for all the common men to see" so they would know he was running for president. Hoover recognized that this pastime helped humanize these self-important men. Fishing, he wrote, "is a constant reminder of the democracy of life, of humility and of human frailty. It is desirable that the President of the United States should be periodically reminded of this fundamental fact—that the forces of nature discriminate for no man." Hoover points out that Harry Truman learned this the hard way while fishing off Key West when his boat was surrounded by sharks.

Jimmy Carter stated in *An Outdoor Journal*: "Growing up as a farm boy, I wanted either a fishing pole or a gun in my hand whenever possible." He refrained from addressing the bizarre story of his solo fishing trip in Georgia in the summer of 1979 when his small boat was attacked by a rabbit. The press had a heyday with the "killer rabbit," with obvious references to the deadly "killer rabbit" from *Monty Python and the Holy Grail*. The *Washington Post* ran a story on its front page the following day about the "banzai bunny" on the fishing trip, saying that the "aquatic attack rabbit . . . was hissing menacingly, its teeth

flashing and nostrils flared, and making straight for the president." More than thirty years later, Carter described the incident to CNN: "A rabbit was being chased by hounds. . . . He jumped in the water and swam toward my boat. When he almost got there, I splashed some water with a paddle." To Carter's credit, he insisted that the story was true, even if politically he would have been wiser to have never mentioned the curious event.

Carter didn't want to release the photographs of the rabid rabbit melee. Perhaps he was wary of how the press reports fishing outings—when a photographer snapped a shot of President Truman holding a fish up in a boat, a journalist later reported that someone else had caught it. "Everyone concedes that the fish will not bite in the presence of the public, including newspapermen," President Hoover warned. Ernest Hemingway agreed that no one should watch while you fish when he wrote, "Somebody just back of you while you are fishing is as bad as someone looking over your shoulder while you write a letter to your girl."

The original outdoorsman president, Teddy Roosevelt, advocated for the "strenuous life" and wouldn't have minded being portrayed in the papers outsmarting a trout. Instead, he honestly described his dangerous adventure wading into a rustling Adirondack stream with black flies and strong current—and not catching a thing. His distant cousin, President Franklin Delano Roosevelt, skipped the photo opportunities and instead fished from a battleship to ease his mind from the toils of the war effort.

This practice of prominent politicians fishing for votes by fishing is not just an American phe-

Calvin Coolidge spent the warmer months fishing at the "Summer White House" along the Brule River in Wisconsin. During the 1920s, the Outdoor Club of Wisconsin designed themed postage stamps that urged voters to "Keep Cool with Coolidge." COURTESY OF THE WISCONSIN HISTORICAL SOCIETY, WHI-44768.

nomenon. Russian president Vladimir Putin often burnishes his image as a macho outdoorsman and wanted to show his fellow countrymen his skills with the rod. His previous stunts included putting down a dangerous tiger with a tranquilizer gun, ripping off his shirt to ride a horse, and flying with a flock of storks. He even dived into the Black Sea in 2011 and miraculously discovered precious artifacts of ancient civilizations. (Only when it was deemed old news did the Kremlin admit it was staged.) In July 2013, Putin visited northern Siberia decked out in shades and camouflage clothes, perhaps to hide from the fish. He allowed a photo op as he petted a reindeer, and then he wanted to haul in a lunker from the lake. Putin's superhuman strength served him well when he revved up a speedboat and proceeded to haul in a forty-six-pound pike. Anglers mocked the obvious ruse by producing doctored photographs showing his

yes-man Prime Minister Dmitry Medvedev in a wet suit attaching the fish to his line, just as Mark Antony had done to impress Cleopatra two millennia before.

The Great Canadian Worm Charming Championship
Fishes' Diet of Worms

Shakespeare showed that worms are just as mighty as the monarch when Hamlet menaces the usurper king Claudius: "A man may fish with the worm that hath eat of a king, and eat of the fish that hath fed of that worm." The English have taken the angst of the bard's most famous character and turned it into a festival. Just as Indian fakirs mesmerize slithering cobras in wicker baskets to dance to the tune of a flute, anglers have "charmed" worms to the surface to be food for the fishes.

Mercutio declared in *Romeo and Juliet* that "they have made worms' meat of me," but anglers want to make worms the meat of fish. The trick of charming these night crawlers into being caught for bait may date back centuries. It's likely that early fishers in search of bait watched birds' and other creatures' techniques of tapping the earth to draw their lunch to the surface.

The bucolic town of Willaston, England, in the hills of Cheshire, sought to give this bizarre practice its proper due. The World Worm Charming Championships began in 1980 to preserve this skill of early English anglers. Following suit, the town of Blackawton in Devon set up its International Festival of

Wormcharming in 1983 with lots of outrageous outfits and the mandatory cakes, crumpets, and scones as scrumptious victuals for the hard-working charmers.

In 2010, Shelburne, Ontario, northwest of Toronto, held its first Canadian Worm Charming Festival, bringing this tradition to the New World. The local newspaper, the Orangeville *Banner*, described the participants who "came armed with sticks, garden forks, iron rods, pitchforks, wooden two by fours, hand saws, hammers—one participant even brandished an Australian didgeridoo last year—and mapped out a three by three metre plot of land." One team of experimental charmers even brought a giant garden fork and hooked it up to a satellite dish, perhaps thinking that interplanetary vibrations would attract the worms to their master.

The trick is to vibrate the earth and make the worms rise to the surface. Despite modern technology, the most successful way of coaxing worms to the surface is by sinking a classic large, four-tine garden fork six inches into the ground and then "twanging" it so vibrations wiggle the earth and the worms slither up. Another technique is called "fiddling," in which a wooden stake is jabbed into the ground and an old saw is "played" against the wooden shaft to attract the worms beneath the surface. Wetting the ground is usually prohibited in competitive matches, but some charmers swear that worms can't resist properly brewed tea or fresh beer.

Many contenders entice exorbitant numbers of worms from the ground in a short amount of time, so the International Federation of Charming Worms and Allied Pastimes of Cheshire, England, created eighteen rules for these high-stake competitions and translated them into thirty languages in hopes of international competition. The world record was set in 1980 by Tom Shufflebotham, the son of a Willaston farmer, who convinced 511 worms to come to the surface in half an hour. This record stood for twenty-nine years, until a ten-year-old girl from England, a Miss Smith, enticed 567 worms to the surface in thirty minutes. The judges award a "golden rampant worm" trophy to the victor. Just as Hamlet held the exhumed jester's skull and questioned his existence, so the worm charmer can place the prize on the mantel as proof of victory over worms. Eventually we will all be food for worms, but in the meantime let's feed the fish a diet of worms with a barbed hook.

Fish Clubs

Aquavit and *Torsk*

"Bring on the *torsk*!" yell the members of Saga Klubben in Bloomington, Minnesota, when they are ready for fresh cod to be served at their Norwegian luncheon club. Occasionally, the group will allow something besides fish, especially to please the ladies when the wives agree to come to their meetings. These men gather together once a month to eat cod and are hardly the only group that does this. In fact, Saga Klubben is a relative newcomer; it formed in 1973 because the waiting list to join other clubs became so long.

These Scandinavian clubs generally opt out of the plentiful freshwater fish in their midst and instead stick with traditional *torsk*, or cod, just as their forefathers ate. The oldest running Scandi-

The Norwegian Fish Club of Los Angeles is one of several Scandinavian luncheon groups along the West Coast. Others are located in San Diego, San Francisco, and Seattle.

navian luncheon league is probably the Norwegian Fish Club of San Francisco, dating to 1914 and now letting women, or "mermaids," join the luncheons. More recent clubs are the Norwegian Fish Club of San Diego and Fiskeklubben of Salt Lake City, which serves no alcohol.

A group of Norwegian masons from the Odinian Society in Seattle formed the Norwegian Commercial Club in 1932, and all the fishermen in the group pushed for a *fiskernes aften*, or "fishermen's evening,"

with the fresh catch of the day. Eventually, the meetings moved to Ballard, the Norwegian neighborhood of Seattle, and they always begin with a happy hour, preferably with aquavit.

The oldest running club dedicated exclusively to cod, the Torske Klubben, began in 1933 in Minneapolis and hasn't changed its menu since then: a giant slab of boiled Atlantic cod, a huge boiled potato, Norwegian flatbread with butter, and a shot or two of Linie aquavit because "the fish has to swim." Members can spoon drawn butter over the cod and potato. "This is the dessert," one of the members told me as he scooped up the butter. The size of the dining hall at Interlachen Country Club in Edina, Minnesota, limits Torske Klubben to about two hundred members. Several other fish clubs popped up to host the hungry Scandinavians who couldn't get in. Norske Torske Klubben regularly seats three hundred members with a less formal atmosphere and boasts that it is the "World's Greatest Torske Klubb," and quite possibly it is the largest such club in the world. Chicago and Madison each have codfish clubs and sent their presidents to the seventy-fifth anniversary of the original Minnesota Torske Klubben, on which they were based.

In response to the boisterous Norwegian luncheon clubs, the Danes formed a club to serve *rødspætte*, a fish in the flounder family that is deep-fried and served with coleslaw, boiled potatoes, and dessert. Rødspætteklub began meeting at the Germanic-American Institute on prestigious Summit Avenue in St. Paul, and "the fact that it is prepared by German Americans is no hindrance," according to the *Minnesota Ethnic Food Book*. Once the Danish *akvavit*

Proudly sailing through the Ballard neighborhood, the Norwegian Commercial Club of Seattle shows its Nordic roots in 1948. The club still meets regularly at the Leif Erikson Lodge for fish dinners amid murals of brave Vikings. PHOTOGRAPH COURTESY OF THE *POST-INTELLIGENCER* COLLECTION, SEATTLE MUSEUM OF HISTORY AND INDUSTRY.

The original logo of the Minneapolis Torske Klubben draws inspiration from the tradition of Norwegian fishing culture.

flowed, the singing and toasts began, and all was good.

Tired of men having all the fun once a month on Saturdays, the wives of the members of the original Torske Klubben wanted a club of their own made up of "women who swim against the current." Lakselaget, or "the Salmon Team," formed in 2002 with a menu of Atlantic salmon, healthy vegetables, and a light dessert, while the men met across town eating boiled white fish and white potato on a white plate. When I asked why Lakselaget didn't serve the traditional cod and aquavit like Torske Klubben, the president replied, "Because salmon and white wine are better."

The original Torske Klubben is steeped in tradition and is proud that the menu and customs have remained unchanged since 1933. Norwegian writer and historian Odd Lovoll points out in *The Promise of America* that Torske Klubben had a precursor, Odin's Club, which celebrated the "'high life' with exclusive banquets at the West Hotel in Minneapolis." For a while, the club met at Camelot, a King Arthur–themed restaurant in a Minneapolis suburb that was designed as a castle with a moat and tin suits of armor inside. A suit and tie were required, as opposed to other fish clubs that settle for informal Norwegian sweaters. "One assumes that they are socially above the members of lodges of the Sons of Norway, with their historically working-class composition," wrote Lovoll. "The members came together to celebrate their Norwegianness and their worldly success. . . .

A large peeled potato, boiled cod, and plenty of drawn butter compose the menu at the Viking Luncheon Club in 1964. Plenty of aquavit and strong black coffee help keep these Scandinavians content. PHOTOGRAPH BY ARTHUR HAGER, *MINNEAPOLIS TRIBUNE*. COURTESY OF THE MINNESOTA HISTORICAL SOCIETY.

At one point this club boasted half the Minnesota Supreme Court as members." Along with the judges, the membership consists of business leaders, university presidents, architects, and prominent politicians. Member Walter Mondale told me, "Hubert Humphrey said, 'If you want to get elected in this state, you have to go to Torske Klubben!'" No wonder it's not uncommon to see the county sheriff accompanied by his honor guard and the visiting members of the Norwegian National Guard.

"The Boss," Bob Gisvold, jokes about the supposedly democratic elections for the officers of the club. "We follow 'Robert's Rules of Order,' and, well, I'm Robert." The Boss bangs his gavel and the festivities begin with a rousing version of "The Star-Spangled Banner" and end with the Norwegian national anthem, "Ja, vi elsker dette landet." One visiting Norwegian, doubting that the cod would be as tasty as back home, told me, "We'll see if the fish is so good!" The native Norwegians of the club went into the kitchen to teach the chefs the proper way to boil the fish. "Last time, they didn't melt the butter correctly," one member told me. "The oily part separated and the Norwegians were very upset. They've overseen every step of the process this time."

To accompany the fish, shot glasses contain ice-cold Linie aquavit, a hard liquor that has traveled over the equator twice in sherry casks. The aquavit-pouring committee circles the room to ensure that everyone's shot glass is filled to the rim—so much so that each time a table is ever so slightly bumped, drops of the golden elixir soak into the tablecloth. The bar used to serve special Norwegian Hansa beer, but the pricey Norwegian kroner put the beer out of reach.

The Boss reminded members, "Please remember to pay your annual dues of one dollar with a slight surcharge of 124 dollars for the aquavit." At the reception counter, the treasurer joked when one member paid his dues, "Is this a tip?" The member quipped, "Maybe in Sweden they would tip, but I'm Norwegian!"

The requisite Sven and Ole jokes typically make Sven the Swede the dim-witted one of the duo. I heard a member tease the Norwegian consul general, who married a Swede. Another member chimed in to his defense: "You know what they call a Swede who married a Norwegian?"

"A mixed marriage," I said.

"No, a social climber."

Members are typically at least half Norwegian, and some worry that offspring who are a quarter Norwegian might not be able to enter. Others joke that the waiting list to become a member is so long that they should enter their children now. "I heard they let a Swede in once," a member said. Were they tricked?

Lutefisk-Eating Contests
Eight Pounds at One Sitting

You know something strange is happening in a town when residents race outhouses on wheels with one person "driving" on the toilet seat. And who are those men dressed in drag for the Ms. Lutefisk Pageant? Are they making fun of the Miss Madison program from the night before?

You know you've entered Madison, Minnesota, after you pass the twenty-five-foot codfish guarding this town on the western prairie. Even though Madison is as landlocked as possible from cold North Atlantic breeding grounds, it boasts the largest cod in the world, which used to travel to towns in the area to promote all things fishy. The "Lou T. Fisk" statue eventually gave up its rambling life and settled on a stone base to welcome visitors to town. Its roaming days weren't over, though: in July 2008 a windstorm blew poor Lou off its pedestal. Fortunately FAST Cor-

This giant codfish statue, Lou T. Fisk, guards the entrance to the very Norwegian town of Madison, Minnesota. The town hosts the annual Norsefest and boasts the world's lutefisk-eating champion. PHOTOGRAPH BY THE AUTHOR.

poration (Fiberglass Animals, Shapes, and Trademarks) in Sparta, Wisconsin, came to the rescue with its master taxidermists to doctor up the fish in time for Madison residents to "praise cod" by dressing him in an officer's outfit for a military parade, Deutsche lederhosen for Oktoberfest, and a fishing getup to be a (cannibalistic?) fisher-fish for the season's fishing opener.

Not only does Madison boast Lou T. Fisk, but cod show up on the town's water tower, and there is a chainsaw sculpture of a lutefisk. This passion for lye-soaked cod extends to several town festivals. Lutefisk Madness is Madison's version of a Crazy Days sidewalk sale. Stinker Days at the end of July feature a three-mile Lou T. Fisk run in which participants are rewarded (or punished) with this Nordic delicacy

Dane County, Wisconsin, is full of Norwegians who opt for cod preserved in lye rather than the fresh fish of the lakes. Tradition rules as these lutefisk connoisseurs wash the caustic chemicals from cod fillets at Ullsvik Grocery Store in Madison, Wisconsin, 1950. PHOTOGRAPH BY ARTHUR M. VINJE. COURTESY OF THE WISCONSIN HISTORICAL SOCIETY, WHI-68597.

The Kildall Fish Company of Minneapolis made advertising cards to adorn streetcar interiors in the early twentieth century. "Holiday Cheer in Every Bite!" Really? COURTESY OF THE MINNESOTA STREETCAR MUSEUM.

after they cross the finish line. The most important festival is November's Norsefest with its famous lutefisk-eating contest. Local man Jerry Osteraas won the world's title in 1987 and began a nine-year streak as champion. His brother-in-law, Duane Schuette, took the title from him, but Osteraas reclaimed the crown in 2001. After ingesting five pounds of lutefisk, Osteraas claimed the award again in 2012. Both Schuette and Osteraas have tied the world's record

of eight pounds at one sitting—and abided by the retention rule of keeping it down for at least fifteen minutes. Osteraas claims he could reach nine pounds if the rules would let him smother the fish in butter.

Madison has the dubious claim of being the town that eats the most lutefisk per capita. Even with a population as small as fifteen hundred, that is a lot of fish soaked in toxic sodium hydroxide. No wonder it is "Lutefisk Capital, U.S.A."

Ugly Bottom-Feeders

The International Eelpout Festival

Most anglers drop lines through the ice in search of walleye, but thousands of fishers venture on the frozen ice of Leech Lake near Walker, Minnesota, in hopes of snagging what the brochures call the "ugliest fish in the world." Eelpout—slimy, prehistoric-looking fish—are dragged from the bottom of the lake and the bizarre festivities begin.

Every February, in subzero weather, a town of icehouses forms for this beer-propelled event. Pirate flags are raised from roofs, perhaps to attract attention for the Most Representative Shelter award given to the craziest shack on ice. This temporary town on top of the frozen lake even has an "eelpout radio sta-

tion" to interview such dignitaries as the mayor. Cars rev up their engines for the Eelpout 500 race on the slippery lake as people watch the spinouts and hope no one gets hurt too bad. Someone rigs up a sofa on skis pulled behind a snowmobile for the ultimate lounging experience. The Bemidji State University rugby team pays a visit for "eelpout rugby," and an "eelpout curling" contest takes advantage of the one crop that never fails in Minnesota: ice. While this all sounds rather chilly, one group even cuts a giant hole in the ice and plunges into the frigid water for charity in the Polar Pout Plunge.

All of these activities perhaps distract from the real purpose of the event: to catch the most eelpout. "They're disgusting, ill-mannered fish that wrap themselves around your arm like an eel," says Minnesota fisherman Geoff Johnson. "I can't believe anyone actually eats them." Eelpout have many nicknames: burbot, mud blower, gudgeon, spineless catfish, mud shark, ling, mother of eels, maria loch, lush, and wethy. These less-than-complimentary names disguise the fact that these freshwater cod are delicious, even if the contents of these ugly bottom-feeders' stomachs may include plastic, wood chips, and even rocks. No wonder there's a line at the fish fry booth for eelpout nuggets.

With all these hungry eaters fishing through the ice, the elusive eelpout have taken a hit. They spawn in the cold of winter, so global warming has been harsh on their populations. Because the Minnesota Department of Natural Resources has labeled eelpout a rough fish, there is no limit to how many can be caught. The International Eelpout Festival has grown from five hundred attendees in early years to fifteen thousand now, so this once undesirable fish gets harder to find the more the fun continues.

Bullhead Days

Anything Deep-Fried Is Edible

Wisconsin governor George Peck wrote a mock editorial in the *Milwaukee Sun* in 1943 advocating for a fish as the state's symbol: "The bullhead never went back on a friend. . . . It is a fish that is a friend of the poor, and one that will sacrifice itself in the interest of humanity. That is the fish that the state should adopt as its trade mark, and cultivate friendly relations with, and stand by. We allude to the bullhead." Although he portrayed this lowly fish as more noble than the aristocratic whitefish, his mock plea fell on deaf ears. The bullhead was not loved.

Governor Peck should have invoked naturalist Henry David Thoreau, who waxed poetic about bullheads, also known as "horned pout," in *Walden*: "At length you slowly raise, pulling hand over hand, some horned pout squeaking and squirming to the upper air. It was very queer, especially in dark nights, when your thoughts had wandered to vast and cosmogonal themes in other spheres, to feel this faint jerk, which came to interrupt your dreams and link you to nature again." If a diner could eat walleye, why eat bullhead?

In Minnesota, ugly bottom-feeders scoured Sak-

atah Lake with venom-coated spines wiggling like whiskers out of their mouth. Rather than send swimmers running for land when this stinging scourge turned up in the beach area, the town of Waterville pulled them from the lake and fed the masses with loaves and bullheads. Taking advantage of this questionable natural resource, town residents yank anywhere from eight to sixteen thousand of these grumpy-looking fish from otherwise pristine waters. To avoid the stingers, cooks wear thick gloves and heave a sharp cleaver to lop off the whiskered head. Pliers strip skin from the fillet, then they are dunked in a vat of batter and deep-fried in oil. The meat tastes a bit muddy, but nothing a swig of cold beer can't fix. "They don't taste so bad," one of the fish vendors told me. "Once you deep-fry them, you can hardly tell it's bullhead."

Bullheads generally have a more delicate flavor in the beginning of the summer, which is why Waterville wisely chooses early June for the festivities. As part of the party, a queen pageant takes place; the town has prudently steered clear of naming the town beauty the "Bullhead Queen." Since 1964, residents have come together to eat bullheads and perhaps purchase a Bobby the Bullhead doll, bullhead T-shirts, and bullhead windsocks. The festival doubles as a public service project to rid the local lake of these fish that look like small catfish with a fat head and tastebud-filled whiskers. Most weigh less than a pound, but the world-record black bullhead grew to a whopping eight pounds. *The Art of Freshwater Fishing* makes fishing for bullheads seem like the perfect pastime: "An old lawn chair, a cane pole, and a can of angleworms are all a fisherman needs to fill a gunny-

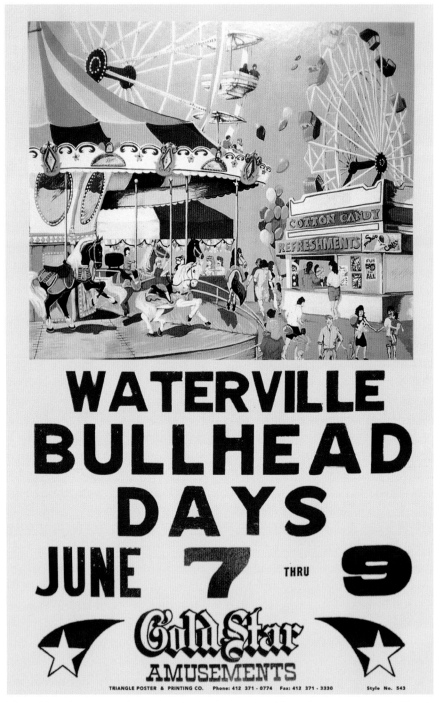

Waterville, Minnesota, makes lemonade from its bitter problem of bottom-feeding bullheads in Sakatah Lake. Each year, the town pulls out thousands of these homely fish and plops them in the deep-fat fryer for a perfect carnival food.

sack with bullheads." In reality, some fishermen will snip their line and lose a lure rather than risk being stung by a bullhead. No wonder the State of Minnesota limits anglers to the nearly impossible catch of one hundred bullheads per day.

Waterville looks on the bright side and views these little fish as an excuse for a party. Who knows? Maybe someday the locals will even mount a bullhead statue, breaded and fried.

Fulda's Fish-O-Rama

Boatloads of Smoked Carp

The most widely eaten fish in the world is also the most popular sport fish across Europe. In Minnesota, the lowly carp does not get royal treatment, except in Fulda.

In 1897, a newspaper from nearby Marshall, the *Warren Sheaf,* condemned Commander Brice of the U.S. Commission of Fish and Fisheries for seeding nearly all the lakes and rivers in the Midwest with this bottom-eating fish: carp's "filth-loving habits foul clear water and impart a muddy, disagreeable taste to its flesh." More than one hundred years later, the *Worthington Daily Globe* applauded the fish that is the reason for Fulda's annual Fish-O-Rama. In 2011, journalist Justine Wettschreck wrote, "Other than a few pickup trucks parked out front, there was little indication that a massive feed was being prepared inside the Larry Pederson Trucking building. Inside, however, board members from the Fulda Game and Fish Club scurried about, scrubbing, cutting, and basting big chunks of fish."

Each year nearly four thousand pounds of carp are seined from nearby West Graham Lake. The carp used to be ordered from elsewhere, but residents prefer the local catch. Game fish are thrown back in the water and these rough fish are hauled into town. "The men spent about six hours cleaning the fish, which truly is about as messy and unappealing as it sounds, they laughed. Fish guts, no matter how much you try to pretty it up, are still fish guts," wrote Wettschreck.

Since 1954, Fulda has gathered for the event, which is canceled if the ice is too thin to net the fish in time for the January fish feed. Originally, fish were cleaned by hand with a hatchet, but a band saw now allows fish to be sliced in a hurry. Once they are cleaned, "We smoke the daylight out of them," Mark Voss said. The diners feast on fish down in the basement, then march upstairs to dance and digest.

Ice Shacks on Main Street

Aitkin's Fish House Parade

Most people shove to get bargains on Black Friday, the day after Thanksgiving, but residents of Aitkin, Minnesota, gather outside in subzero temperatures to watch a bizarre procession of decorated ice shacks meandering down Main Street (Highway 210) on top of trailers, mostly on their way to Lake Mille Lacs for the opening of ice fishing season. Minnesota boasts almost ninety thousand licensed ice shacks, and more than five thousand are carried to the hot spots of Mille Lacs.

The parade began in 1990 when the marketing director of Aitkin's Chamber of Commerce, Chuck Butler, commented, "Well, maybe if you just lined up a bunch of trucks with fish houses in the back,

Just as the making of sausage might not be appetizing but the result is delicious, so too is Fulda's Fish-O-Rama: done right, carp can taste fantastic, and locals much prefer the catch from the nearby lake to fish from elsewhere. PHOTOGRAPH BY JUSTINE WETTSCHRECK / WORTHINGTON *DAILY GLOBE.*

and had a parade, that would be better than what we're doing now." Each year the cavalcade grows with ever wilder and more interesting designs. The local Methodist congregation brings its "Little Church on Ice" shack, which is probably the only chapel in the world with parishioners who walk on water to get to the church on time.

The 2014 parade featured kids dressed as invasive species (milfoil, zebra mussels) to strike terror into the public. If that didn't do the trick, the "Dying to Fish" house blasted Michael Jackson's "Thriller" and had a gang of fishing zombies dancing in the street in parkas, scarves, and Sorel boots. Perhaps most disturbing were the kids leaping into the streets for candy in slush puddles and then gobbling the wet, half-frozen Tootsie Rolls. Fortunately for spectators, the parade moves in slow motion because the heavy ice shacks need to pause at the only stoplight in the county before heading out to the ice. 🐟

Opposite: The beginning of the ice fishing season on Lake Mille Lacs in central Minnesota is marked by the Fish House Parade in Aitkin. Even in subzero temperatures, Minnesota Avenue in Aitkin is filled with creative fish shacks pulled through town on trailers. PHOTOGRAPHS BY THE AUTHOR.

A blazing fire lights up this fish boil at a Wisconsin resort along the shore of Door County in 1967. PHOTOGRAPH BY OLIVER REESE. COURTESY OF THE WISCONSIN HISTORICAL SOCIETY, WHI-38351.

CHAPTER FIVE

Fish Fries and Fish Boils
Smelt, Eelpout, and Pickled Pike

You Americans are always asking, "Does it taste fishy?"
Of course it tastes fishy—it's fish!

—*Norwegian journalist Vigdis Devik*

Friday night means fish fries—just follow your nose to the beer batter splashing in the fryer. A healthier alternative can be found at the weekly fish boils up and down the coast of Lake Superior and Lake Michigan with freshly caught, snake-like "lawyers," or eelpout, right out of the lake. (An even better option to keep the heart pumping is eelpout oil.) Is fish on Friday some sort of Catholic conspiracy? Well, no, but it did inspire the famous Filet-O-Fish at McDonald's.

That's not to say that eating fish isn't political, as shown by Mikhail Gorbachev's famous fish dinner in St. Paul that unofficially put the Cold War to rest. The following pages supply the best beer batter recipe and even highlight the future of ice fishing with delivery of twelve-packs of suds via drone.

Before the refrigerator was invented, hungry diners relied on the fresh haul of the day or found

This lodge along the north shore of Lake Superior advertises its fish fries for visitors in search of a hearty meal right out of the big lake, circa 1947. COURTESY OF THE KATHRYN A. MARTIN LIBRARY, UNIVERSITY OF MINNESOTA DULUTH, ARCHIVES AND SPECIAL COLLECTIONS.

creative ways to preserve fish. Crafty fishermen smoke, salt, pickle, or even marinate and "cure" fish for a few days by putting a rock on top of fresh trout fillets. Dried fish kept indefinitely and was traded almost as easily as currency. If you consider the thousands of dollars that fishermen spend on fishing equipment, you can understand why fish are like gold.

Frying Fish on Friday

A Papal Conspiracy?

Friday night fish fries are inseparable from our culture, but where does this practice come from? Some assume a conspiratorial papal pact between the Holy See and fishermen so the Church could influence this market. Brian Fagan, author of *Fish on Friday*, denounced this theory on National Public Radio: "Many people have searched the Vatican archives on this, but they have found nothing."

Before the Christian tradition of avoiding meat on Friday, the Greeks indulged on a Friday feast day in honor of the fish goddess Aphrodite Salacia, from whom the word "salacious" is derived. The Romans adopted many Greek customs, and the Church likely continued this tradition of eating fish on Friday. The exact origin of the Friday–fish connection is difficult to confirm, leaving some to claim that the Norse namesake for the day, either the goddess Freya or Frigg, also had her feast day on Friday. Fish was inevitably consumed in homage to the goddess.

The Church in Rome had several reasons to recognize fish as holy. According to Genesis, God created fish on the fifth day, which would be Friday if the week starts on Monday. The fish in the sea are constantly baptized, so eating them is a reminder of baptism. Because fish have no eyelids, some claim that these never-closing eyes are a metaphor for God, who always watches over us. Others discuss how Jesus is represented through the symbol of a fish, so this could be viewed as another form of transubstantiation, of literally eating the body of Christ. And Jesus's famous feeding of the multitude was with loaves and fishes, not steak.

Despite no secret accord between the Church and fishermen to forever guarantee sales on Fridays, the Vatican did set down guidelines to avoid eating warm-blooded mammals on Wednesday and Friday and during Advent and Lent. The assumption is that the devout would eat fish, but technically turtles, lizards, and alligators could also be on the list to fry. Snake could be included, too, but that symbolism is too loaded.

To save money, the Church encouraged monks to eat fish. At Christ Church in Canterbury around 1077, a monk would receive much more food if he agreed to eat fish. To discourage decadent meat eating in the monasteries, "in 1336 Pope Benedict XII decreed that at least half the monks in a community must eat in the refectory daily," according to historian Brian Fagan, and only Monday, Tuesday, and Thursday could they eat "irregular foods" such as meat. "Benedict's decrees were widely accepted, even if nominally obeyed."

The papal ruling was further watered down in Britain when Henry VIII broke away from the Vatican in the early 1500s so he could divorce Catherine of Aragon and marry Anne Boleyn. The English diet

In 1880, Walter Dendy Sadler painted *Thursday*, showing a group of monks getting ready for their Friday meal. Around 1077, some English monks would receive a larger ration if they ate more fish.

was full of fish, and there were recommended days for consuming it, but suddenly it became viewed with skepticism as "popish" flesh. Even William Shakespeare makes reference in *King Lear* to these times when eating fish was viewed as a political act. In act 1, scene 4, the character Kent tries to convince King

Opposite: The "World's Largest Fish Fry" was held on Voyageur Day in 1970 along the Canadian border in Crane Lake, Minnesota. COURTESY OF THE MINNESOTA HISTORICAL SOCIETY.

Lear to hire and trust him. Kent promises to "serve him truly that will put me in trust, to love him that is honest . . . to fight when I cannot choose; and to eat no fish." In other words, he is not a Catholic.

Not until 1547 did Henry VIII's son, Edward VI, require fasting days of just fish "for the benefit of the commonwealth" and to help the troubled fishing industry. Oliver Cromwell changed it all back a hundred years later and put a damper on all the Friday night fish fries. Kate Colquhoun, in *Taste: The Story*

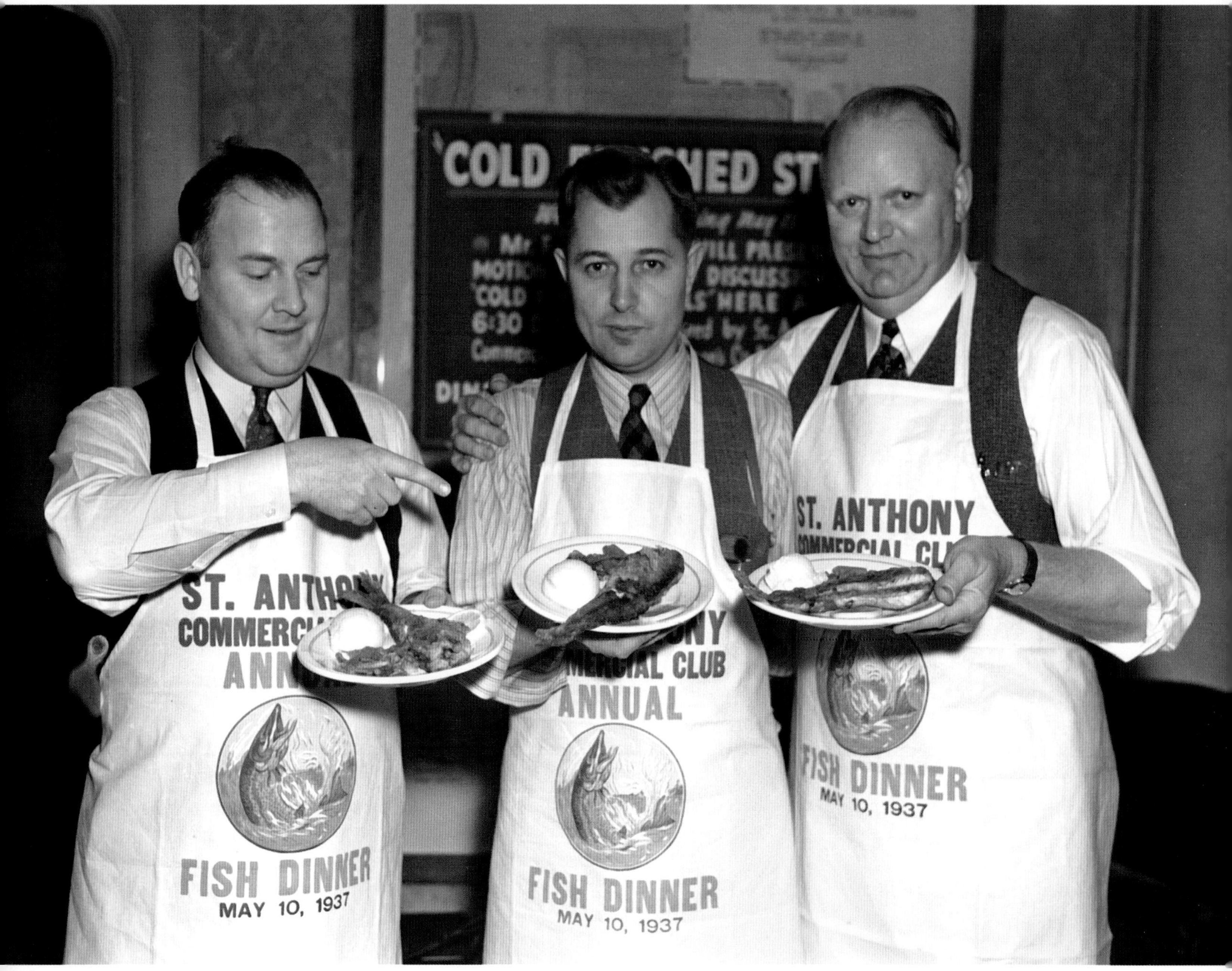
ST. ANTHONY
ANNUAL
FISH DINNER
MAY 10, 1937

of Britain through Its Cooking, describes the times: "Puritans wore stark black with square white collars and linen caps or tall hats, Christmas and celebrations were banned, pleasure was repressed, and fish days and fasting were proscribed as Popish." Nevertheless, fish on Friday persisted in Catholic communities for centuries. In December 2014 in the town of Friendship, Wisconsin, according to Reuters, John Przybyla was pulled over by the police for his tenth drunken offense but cleverly blamed the beer-batter fish fry for the high alcohol content running through his blood.

Another man who successfully took advantage of fish on Fridays was McDonald's franchise owner Lou Groen, whose hamburger stand was located in a Catholic neighborhood of Cincinnati. Groen complained that his sales slumped on Fridays, so McDonald's owner Ray Kroc offered him an alternative: a slice of pineapple on a bun in place of beef. Groen rightly predicted Kroc's pineapple burger would be a disaster and instead offered the first Filet-O-Fish in 1962. His original recipe called for halibut, but economics forced him to use Atlantic cod. In 1966, Pope Paul VI relaxed restrictions for Catholics about eating fish on Fridays, but McDonald's had already struck gold and eventually would sell three hundred million Filet-O-Fish a year, mostly on Fridays.

Fourteen years after the introduction of the Filet-O-Fish in 1962, McDonald's debuted the Phil A. O'Fish mascot. The sandwich's inventor, Lou Groen, originally envisioned tasty halibut as the mystery fish inside, but later settled for cod and then Alaskan pollock. COLLECTION OF JASON LIEBIG.

Fish Boils

First We Kill All the Lawyers!

Cauldrons of boiling water perfectly cooking fresh fish are a tradition on the Lake Michigan coastline of Wisconsin, stemming primarily from Icelandic commercial fishers. On Washington Island on the tip of Door County, I arrive hungry to a summer fish boil arranged by one of the few remaining commercial fishermen in the area, Ken Koyen, a Danish American owner of K. K. Fiske Restaurant. He runs two of the last three fish tugs on the island and hauls his fish back to the restaurant, a building with a section that dates to 1860.

A sign announcing "Fish Boil Tonight" is raised in front of his restaurant every Wednesday, Friday, and Saturday during the summer months. A giant black kettle with gallons of steaming water bubbles away, filled with onions, carrots, and potatoes cooking over a crackling fire. Koyen places the fresh fillets into the boiling brine and waits several minutes. He tosses a cup of kerosene on the flames. "Great balls of fire!" someone shouts as a blazing flash engulfs the pot, causing the salty liquid to boil over and douse the flames. Dinner is ready.

The menu varies depending on the catch, so Koyen explains that tonight we will be eating perch and lawyers. "What?" I ask. "Lawyers?"

I examine the printed menu that describes burbot, or eelpout: "[Washington] Islanders named it 'lawyer' because the location of the heart is in its Gluteus Max!" T-shirts sold at the bar ask "Got Lawyers?" as a spoof of milk advertisements and "Fresh Lawyers" is painted on the picture window with a colored drawing of the slithery fish. These aggressive snake-like fish are freshwater cod and are also called spineless catfish, lota lota, gudgeon, mudblowers, or mother eel. Even the guide on the Cherry Train Tour around the island describes lawyers over the intercom (with little kids present): "They have a very small heart very close to their anus."

Fishing for Buffalo questions the unusual nickname of "lawyers," "Some speculate its name comes from the burbot's slimy, eel-like tail, which wraps around your arm when you pick it up. Others guess it refers to the burbot's high intelligence or aggressive behavior." The authors called the president of the South Dakota Bar Association for insight, who responded, "My guess would be that the name comes from the fact that, like lawyers, the burbot works extremely hard and is often undervalued in society." When asked if the name derives from the slimy eel-like appearance, the human lawyer replied, "I can't imagine there would be any connection." Regardless of etymology, the waitress delivers a perfect plate of filleted lawyers to my table. The delicate, delectable fish is flaky and delicious, especially with a generous dollop of butter. Burbot deserves its other nickname: the poor man's lobster.

The second fish boil I attend is far inland at the tourist hotspot of Wisconsin Dells. Past the fudge stands, exploding volcanoes, monster truck rides, and UFO museums, the Thunder Valley Inn stands as a pastoral Scandinavian-themed oasis a couple miles outside town. This old farm has several wooden buildings around the gravel turnabout and a gazebo for outdoor concerts. The reception area doubles as a gift shop, with berry syrups for sale next to Ole and Lena joke books. Through the strings of little Scan-

Eelpout, or burbot, are known as "lawyers" in Door County, Wisconsin. On nearby Washington Island, they say that the name is because "they are ugly bottom-feeders." K. K. Fiske Restaurant features weekly fish boils in the summer—and first they eat all the lawyers. PHOTOGRAPH BY THE AUTHOR.

dinavian flags dangling from the rafters, we see that everyone is gathered in the restaurant for a fish feast. The waitresses shuffling around the tables sport Norwegian dresses with frilly aprons, head scarves, and puffy white shirts. An older woman, perhaps the owner, sees us and says, "You're just in time for the fish boil!"

Katy, my pregnant wife, looks at me with both

DOOR COUNTY Fish Boil

BRING 15 GAL. WATER TO RAPID BOIL OVER LARGE OUTDOOR FIRE. ADD 4 LBS. SALT AND 7 LBS. BUTTER. WHEN BOIL RESUMES ADD 150 DOOR COUNTY NEW POTATOES; BOIL 14 MIN. ADD 100 SMALL ONIONS; BOIL 2 MIN. ADD 50 LBS. FRESH LAKE MICHIGAN WHITEFISH; BOIL 10 MIN. CREATE BOIL OVER. DRAIN AND SERVE WITH BUTTER.

Classic

Recipe

Up and down the Lake Michigan coast in Wisconsin, fish boils mean summer. Fifty pounds of fresh fish indicates a big party. The secret ingredient? Seven pounds of butter.

pleading and anger because of where I've brought her. Boiled whitefish does not satisfy her cravings. "I'll just have a salad," she tells the waitress.

I order the fish boil and see that the mitigating factor to boiled fish, since it is not fried, is a cup of drawn butter poured over the top. To help me digest, the waitress advises, "We recommend Uff-da Beer. It's made in Wisconsin but with an Old World recipe." Someone describes the taste—and alcohol—as three Budweisers condensed into one twelve-ounce beer. The strong ale combined with the music of a yodeling polka band adds to the ambience of the fish boil. The waitress tells us that Friday night fish boils are a dancing party. "It's time to grab a partner!" the bandleader announces. "Let's do the Chicken Dance!" This sends a ripple effect around the half dozen tables in the restaurant; diners leave their half-eaten fish and cooks come out of the kitchen to get everyone on the dance floor.

Katy crosses her arms and says, "I am not, I repeat not, dancing the Chicken Dance." She reminds me that she is not at all Scandinavian so she has no obligation to stand up and jiggle like a pregnant hen. Never mind that the Chicken Dance is a Wisconsin tradition based on an old German polka.

In tempo with the accordion, the dancers tap their fingers together like a chicken beak, wave their arms like an angry bird, and wiggle their Norwegian rears in rhythm. The song ends with booming applause from the crowd, and everyone returns to their buttery fish. The hostess brings over another Uff-da and says, slightly out of breath, "Whew, that was a lot of fun! They usually play it again in the next set so you'll have another chance." Katy explains that we've had a long day and need to get up early tomorrow. The waitress is disappointed but stays upbeat. *"Tusen takk,"* she says as she hands us the bill for the fish with a smile. "That means 'thank you' in Norwegian."

Fish boils in Door County, Wisconsin, have changed little over the years. Just boil a cauldron of water and add fresh fish. After ten minutes, add kerosene to the fire for a mini fireball that causes the pot to boil over and douse the flames.

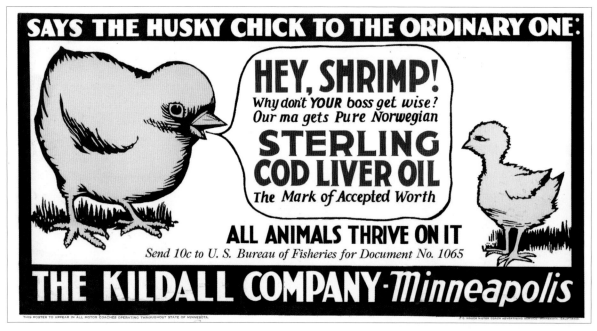

The large number of Norwegian immigrants to the upper Midwest brought the tradition of giving cod-liver oil to kids, as promoted here in this advertisement from the Kildall Fish Company of Minneapolis in the 1930s. COURTESY OF THE MINNESOTA HISTORICAL SOCIETY.

Eelpout Oil

Elixir of the Gods

A Norwegian immigrant to Wisconsin was worried about the American diet around the turn of the past century. "The large amount of pork that Americans eat is not good for people unaccustomed to such a heavy diet. . . . Our farmers from uplands think it is a fine food, but in a warm climate, used in excess, it is very injurious, especially when eaten without an abundance of vegetables," according to *Norwegians in Wisconsin*. In other words, to be healthy, eat more fish!

Scandinavians complained about the large quantities of meat consumed in the United States and dubbed it the reason for disease (and perhaps future obesity). Eighty percent of Scandinavians live within a dozen miles of the sea, so fish is essential to their diet. The Inuit keep healthy through massive amounts of fish, or, as *Fishing for Buffalo* states, "Eskimos, who eat lots of whitefish, have one of the lowest rates of heart disease of any people, even though they eat huge quantities of fat." The southern world viewed these northerners as bizarre "oil drinkers" because of their strange habit of taking doses of fish oil for health.

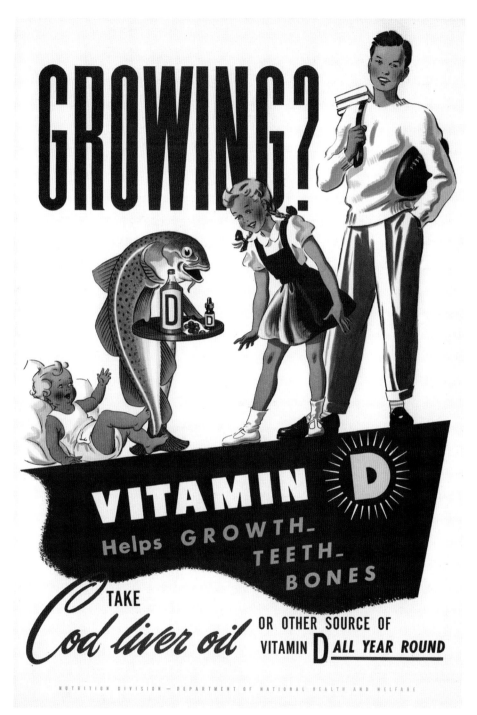

Full of Vitamins A and D, cod-liver oil prevents rickets and keeps kids healthy. Scandinavian mothers spooned the fishy oil into squeamish young mouths during the winter months, though the Canadian Department of Health and Welfare advocated ingesting the oil year-round. COURTESY OF THE LIBRARY AND ARCHIVES OF CANADA.

Theodore Rowell, seen here in his laboratory, devised a system to extract mineral-rich oil from the eelpout his family caught in Lake of the Woods in northern Minnesota. COURTESY OF THE ROWELL FAMILY ARCHIVES; REPRINTED WITH PERMISSION.

During the long, dark winters, Scandinavian immigrants and the Inuit would take cod-liver oil as a cure for just about anything: rheumatism to rickets, tuberculosis to lung trouble. In 1928, the Nobel Committee awarded Adolf Windaus its chemistry prize for decoding the molecular structure of vitamin D and the role that cod-liver oil can play in relieving rickets, sometimes called the "English disease."

Land-locked farmers or even fishers on freshwater lakes didn't have easy access to those good omega-3 oils hidden in the livers of ocean cod. During World War II, the price of Norwegian cod-liver oil soared to almost $145 a barrel before it became completely unavailable. Ted Rowell of remote Roseau, Minnesota, made a million-dollar discovery deep in the depths of Lake of the Woods. In the 1920s, Rowell's family netted for walleyes on Lake of the Woods but mostly caught slimy eelpout, often called burbot *(lota masculosa)*. "Commercial fishermen, who ply their operations in Lake of the Woods border waters, long considered burbot worthless. They have dumped untold thousands of these fish on the lake shores to rot," according to a *Popular Mechanics* article on Rowell in March 1947. The Rowells didn't want the fish to go to waste, so they fed them to arctic foxes on their farm. When they observed that the foxes developed shinier, thicker fur, they found out there was magic in eelpout.

Ted Rowell had graduated from the University of Minnesota School of Pharmacy but didn't have high-tech equipment in northwestern Minnesota in the 1920s. He cut out eelpout livers, extracted the oil, and started experiments on his kitchen cookstove. The eelpouts' livers are six times bigger than most other freshwater fish and almost 10 percent of their body weight, enabling them to potentially survive up to four months without eating. The oil had four to eight times the amount of vitamins A and D that imported Norwegian cod-liver oil had, and it was more easily digested by humans. Eelpout is freshwater cod, a distant relative of the giant schools of cod in the Atlantic; ages ago, after ocean waters receded, many of the cod were likely stuck in inland lakes, adapted to freshwater, and survived.

Rowell began to extract the oil and sell it under the name of Rowell Laboratories out of Baudette, Minnesota. To keep children from getting rickets during the Great Depression, eelpout oil was offered free to many impoverished children by the humanitarian Mary Evelyn C. Smith. Fish oil, along with a healthy dose of sunshine, was recommended for babies to help them survive the dark winter and increase their brainpower. Burbot oil was all the rage to keep kids healthy. Today, doctors in the United States are again recognizing the benefits of fish oil and prescribing a daily dose to many patients.

When the Nazis marched on Norway, shipments of cod-liver oil were completely cut off to North America, and business boomed in Baudette. "In 1940 Rowell handled a half million pounds of burbot in his laboratories and the over-all total now is about five million pounds from Lake of the Woods alone," a *Popular Mechanics* article titled "Vitamin Harvest" said in 1947. "Burbot livers are also shipped to Rowell from as far east as the Great Lakes and from other regions." Because Rowell caught so many burbot in Lake of the Woods, the number of game fish increased by half. "Rowell's vitamin industry is

Rowell displays a freshly caught burbot, its liver bloated with the profitable oil that made Rowell a household name in the vitamin business. COURTESY OF THE ROWELL FAMILY ARCHIVES; REPRINTED WITH PERMISSION.

as highly praised by sportsmen as it is by medical scientists."

Now, decades later, there is interest in rediscovering this restorative tincture, which is not currently available on the market. The *Mille Lacs Messenger* from August 30, 2012, recognized that "eelpout oil

sold particularly well because all other fish oils in the market required spoonfuls per dosage, whereas eelpout oil only required three drops." In 1990, *Fishing for Buffalo* stated, "Burbot liver, like cod liver, is rich in vitamins A and D. Currently, tests are being conducted to see if burbot liver oil can be used in ointments as is cod liver oil." Eelpout has been listed as a rough fish, so the Minnesota Department of Natural Resources hasn't kept track of how many were caught, and there is no limit. Because of this bountiful resource, Chris Niskanen wrote in the *St. Paul Pioneer Press* on April 26, 1999, "One commercial fishing operation on Lake of the Woods turned eelpout into medicinal oil at a rate of six gallons an hour." Perhaps eelpout elixir is back.

Lynne Rossetto Kasper's Sweet/Sour Icehouse Fish Stew

The St. Paul–based radio show *The Splendid Table* has brought international cooking to the land of tuna hotdish. Lynne Rossetto Kasper offers a recipe beyond Friday fish fries that is perfect for free eelpout. She wrote: "As an adopted Minnesotan I think of our local fish, and what comes to mind immediately are icehouses and the great (and seemingly somewhat lunatic, to the outlander I was thirty years ago when we first came to Minnesota) tradition of not letting a mere thirty inches of ice get between us and our lake fish." She recommends, "Almost anything you catch yourself or find at the market can go into this stew. To not overcook the fish, add it just before serving, with thicker slices going in maybe two minutes before thinner ones."

¼ cup good-tasting extra virgin olive oil, or a mix of oil and butter

3 medium onions, cut into ½-inch dices

1 large sweet red pepper, cut into ½-inch dices (optional)

Salt to taste

½ to 1 teaspoon fresh ground black pepper

2 large garlic cloves, minced

½ teaspoon dry thyme

1 teaspoon each dry oregano and ground allspice

1 tablespoon dry basil

⅛ teaspoon hot red pepper flakes

3 tablespoons red wine vinegar, or to taste

½ cup dry white wine

1 28-ounce can whole peeled tomatoes

1½ cups broth (vegetable or chicken) or water

3 tablespoons raisins

1 to 3 teaspoons of sugar (optional)

2 pounds filleted fish (walleye, perch, eelpout, trout, cod, halibut) cut into 1-inch pieces

1. In a six- to eight-quart pot, heat oil over medium-high heat. Stir in onions and sweet pepper with salt and black pepper. Cook until golden. Blend in garlic, herbs, pepper, vinegar, and wine. Cook down until almost no liquid is left.

2. Stir in tomatoes and broth. Simmer, covered, for twenty minutes. Stir in raisins and cook another five minutes uncovered. Taste for seasoning; add salt and pepper and/or vinegar and sugar to get a well-seasoned, sweet–tart balance.

3. Maintain the stew at a slow bubble. Slip in the thickest pieces of fish. Cook one minute and add the thinner cuts. Cook just until firm (maybe thirty seconds). Ladle the stew into bowls. Rice or stubby noodles taste great with the stew, as does beer.

Paul Bunyan and Sourdough Sam at the Escanaba Smelt Jamboree, Escanaba, Michigan

OB-H993

Smelt fries like Michigan's Escanaba Smelt Jamboree are popular events throughout the north woods, even attracting folk heroes like Paul Bunyan and Sourdough Sam. COLLECTION OF DONALD HARRISON.

Grilled Fingerlings

Whoever Smelt It

One of the few fish that can be netted legally, smelt run in the early spring. In the wee hours of the morning, fishers fill buckets upon buckets of these little fish that they spot with a headlamp. Some stuff the back of their pickups with wiggling smelt and bring them to town for a fish fry. The hazing ritual for rookies new to the world of smelt calls for them to bite the head off one of the poor little minnows. The rest of the catch are decapitated (with knives), gutted, and usually dunked in beer batter (scales and all) for finger food.

Dan Eastman, the lead chef at Concordia Language Villages in Bemidji, went smelting with his dad in Duluth starting when he was just four years old. They loaded the bed of a pickup truck with five-gallon buckets filled with smelt, and he played with the flopping fish before filling up on them. Rather than the typical deep-fried version, Eastman remembers skewering them to grill.

Opposite: Most smelt are deep-fried and eaten whole, but it's even better to grill them for a succulent and healthy dinner. PHOTOGRAPH BY TIM WOJCIK.

Dan Eastman's Grilled Smelt

36 fresh smelt

salt

pepper

36 small skewers

Depending on how squeamish you are, smelt can be grilled whole or their little heads can be cut off and the innards pulled out. The bones can be left in, and there is no need to scale them. Run a skewer through each one lengthwise, and grill about four minutes per side without letting them fall through the grate. Charcoal is best, but a gas grill will work. Serves four.

Fish as Money

Pickled Pike and Herring

Herring was called the "silver of the sea" by Scandinavians, and dried cod was essentially used as currency since it would keep indefinitely and always promised a good fish dinner when reconstituted. Herring choker nets extended throughout the Great Lakes to catch ciscoes, or lake herring, to satisfy Scandinavian immigrants' hankering for pickled fish. At a historical museum on Washington Island on Lake Michigan, Pam Goodlet's book of recipes from her grandma recommends pickling just about anything to keep it from spoiling—fish, of course, but she also recommends pickling beef heart and tongue.

The Scandinavians on this island and elsewhere on the coasts of the Great Lakes took advantage of the abundance of the smaller fish to make all sorts of creative recipes that they brought from the Old World. *Sildesalat* is Norwegian herring salad, typically made with beets, potatoes, onions, and pickled herring, and the Finns add apples to make *rosolli*. Pickled herring was typically a breakfast treat, while mashed fish with egg and bread crumbs makes a dinner of herring cakes. This love for herring is so pronounced in Norway that two towns, Florø and Haugesund, compete for the "world's longest herring table" and feed fish to as many as thirty thousand diners, with many sauces (including mustard dill, red wine, and juniper berries) to choose from.

With herring as a dietary staple, Scandinavians panicked in 1549 when the giant schools of herring did not appear for the annual catch. Convinced that Providence was punishing his immoral citizens, King Christian III of Denmark and Norway issued a decree: "Since there is danger that God may withdraw his blessing on account of the great sins and vices of inhabitants of the coasts, our tax gatherers, each one in his own district, shall see to it that the people in the fishing stations lead good and Christian lives." A decade later, the herring returned to the fishermen's nets and obedient prayer and careful compliance to the Bible was credited.

Fishermen following schools of fish across the Atlantic are credited by some historians as the reason Vikings made it to Newfoundland and perhaps beyond. Some Scandinavian-centric scholars claim that when the Vikings turned to Christianity, they paid "in form of peltry and fish; the tax lists, now in the Vatican in Rome, show there were at least one thousand families in the American colonies in the twelfth century." That remains to be confirmed.

This small statue in front of a Norwegian *stabbur* in Westby, Wisconsin, shows a *nisse* named Ole bringing a gift of fish. Although the writing on the statue claims it's a lutefisk, the little fellow's apron would be more slimy if that were the case.
PHOTOGRAPH BY THE AUTHOR.

101. *Fiskedrager fra Bergen.*

Fish netted in northern waters could be so large that Norwegian fisherman would drag their profitable catch to market. PHOTOGRAPH BY MARCUS SELMER, CIRCA 1860-70. COURTESY OF THE NATIONAL LIBRARY OF NORWAY.

With the immense stock of fish in the Great Lakes, Scandinavians, especially Norwegians and Icelanders, began intense netting. The Finns were accustomed to *silakka,* herring or sprat from the Baltic Sea, but soon lake herring, smelt, or even northern pike and walleye were substituted in Finnish recipes. Today, much of the caviar from Lake Superior herring isn't appreciated by Americans and is sent from the Dockside Fish Market in Grand Marais to Morey's in Motley and off to Sweden, Norway, and Finland, where these precious eggs are gobbled up.

When fish stock in the Great Lakes dried up because of heavy netting and the introduction of invasive species, fish enthusiasts were forced to look elsewhere for dinner. Northern pike, which are abundant in smaller freshwater lakes, proved a fine substitute for herring since the "floating" bones melt away with the vinegar. This recipe for pickled fish from avid northwoods fisherman Jim Mundt was told to him by Al LeVasseur of Dixon Lake.

Pickled Northern Pike

First Cycle

Cut fish in 1-inch pieces, thin, about ¼ inch thick; put fish in plastic container with cover.

Add ⅝ cup canning salt per quart of fish.

Cover fish and salt with white vinegar; let stand in refrigerator six days. Stir fish every day to dissolve salt.

After six days start second cycle.

Second Cycle

Wash fish in cold water until water is clear.

Cut five or six onions in round slices.

Alternate layers of fish and layers of onions in plastic bowl. Fish and onions should make a 5-quart batch when done.

Add 2 or 2½ cups sugar to fish and onions, depending on desired sweetness.

Add 1 quart white port wine (or any sweet white wine).

Add enough white vinegar to cover fish and onions. Lemon slices or lemon juice can also be added (optional).

Add ⅓ cup whole pickling spices. Keep refrigerated and stir every day.

After six days put fish in jars, cover with juice, and seal.

Keep refrigerated. This makes a four-quart batch of pickled pike.

Preserving Fish

Smoked, Dried, or Fermented

Once a fish is caught, the fun begins. If the catch isn't released, what is the best way to cook it? If it can't be consumed immediately, how can it be preserved? The book *Fishing for Buffalo* gives gruesome details about cleaning carp: "When it's time to go home, kill the fish by knocking it on the head. Chop off the head and tail, draining out as much blood as possible. Split the belly, pull out the entrails and gills, and wash the blood from the body cavity."

When cleaning pike, my Swedish grandmother encouraged, "Whack it on the head with a paddle! Then it won't feel anything so you can cut its head off." I always thought this was cruel, but then I read in *Fishing for Buffalo* that Mike Walker from the Louisiana Department of Wildlife and Fisheries recommended cleaning gar with a hatchet, baseball bat, and tin snips: "Hit him over the head with a hammer where the scales meet the head. That usually settles him down."

Norwegians talk about wanting their fish *blod-fersk*, or blood-fresh. Friends from northern Norway told me about a fisherman they knew on the North Sea who kept a pot of water boiling on his trawler since he would only eat fish within the hour it was caught—otherwise he considered it foul. However, in Norway's past, fresh food was viewed by many as potentially unhealthy. Meats and fish were usually salted for preservation and to kill dangerous bacteria. Creative Scandinavians boiled, buried, dried, pickled, or soaked fish in lye.

Smoked whitefish is arguably the tastiest treat in the Midwest, and dozens of smoke shacks along the Great Lakes serve this specialty to visitors. Another popular technique for fish preservation is with vinegar and sugar to prevent bacteria from seeping in. Mexican ceviche is essentially the same idea, fresh

Not all fresh fish could make it to market in time, so whitefish and trout were smoked to lengthen their shelf life. Besides, smoked fish is delicious. Here employees at Sam Johnson and Sons pack freshly smoked herring in Duluth in 1949. COURTESY OF THE MINNESOTA HISTORICAL SOCIETY.

The immigrant tradition of drying fish was brought to the Midwest by Norwegian fishermen from areas above the Arctic Circle, where the climate was perfectly dry and cool enough for the fish to become *klippefisk*. This photograph is from a spit of land near the town of Svolvær in the Lofoten Islands. PHOTOGRAPH BY THE AUTHOR.

fish "cooked" with lime, and the Tavern on Grand in St. Paul uses freshwater walleye for its delicious ceviche with avocado and cilantro.

Scandinavians traditionally prepared *gravlaks* by wrapping and burying cured salmon. Now the salmon is typically smothered in salt, sugar, and sometimes dill, and a heavy object is placed on top of the wrapped fillets to "cure" it for a few days. A

Salt cod was a staple that would keep indefinitely and could be a great dinner when other food wasn't available. Just soak the fish overnight, and it's ready to cook. With modern refrigeration, salt fish is less common since fresh fish is preferred. PHOTOGRAPH BY THE AUTHOR.

lighter version of fermented fish is known as *rakør-ret,* or fermented trout. A Norwegian explained the surprising system to me: "The fishermen take a trout, smother it in salt and sugar, and bury it underground for three to four months. As soon as the whole town stunk like rotting fish, the hungry villagers would simply follow their noses to the hidden treasures. You must be careful not to touch the fish, or the bacteria from your hands can infect it." The fermented fish is very flavorful but can be risky to eat. Almost every year someone gets very sick from it in Norway around Christmastime.

Rather than burying their fish, many commercial fishermen relied on the outdoor elements for preservation. According to the North Shore Commercial Fishing Museum, fishermen would strew fish on the dock and let them freeze. Children waved seagulls away until the catch was sufficiently frozen. Avid fisherman Jake Cline recalls fishing in the winter near Hackensack, Minnesota, in *Classic Minnesota Fishing Stories*: "It was awfully cold, and when I threw 'em out of the fish house they froze. Then I stacked 'em up in my arms and carried 'em to the pickup. When I got to town it was about 10 o'clock. They were just getting ready to close up at the Chat 'n' Chew restaurant. I made a couple of trips to the pickup and carried those crappies inside there to show 'em."

One preservation technique that has been popular for thousands of years is drying fish carcasses on large wooden racks. Dried fish were essential for the Vikings to be able to travel far and wide, wreaking havoc. I traveled to the Lofoten Islands in Norway, where locals have dried fish for hundreds of years on thirty-foot A-framed racks on fingers of land that stretch into the North Sea. I watched a fishing boat approach a nondescript cement building along the shore, and the fishermen unloaded beautiful fish (and then beheaded them and pulled out their entrails). The meat of the cod was hung out to make *tørrfisk* (dried fish), which easily keeps for twenty years and would be shipped around the world. Cod tongues were a delicacy, and even the heads were dried for fish stock. Immigrant Gudrun Lindal Magnusson talked about *tørrfisk* in *Scandinavian Family Album*: "And then the hard fish. That wasn't really considered as a food, but a delicacy. Hard fish is cod, dried cod, dried so you have to beat it to be able to chew it."

Salted fish is another method of preservation, but it requires a large amount of salt and a secure place to keep animals away from the fish as the water is wicked away. Just as the Vikings carried dried or salted fish, many immigrants kept this hard fish on hand for an easy supper. Minnesotan hunter and fisherman Jamie Carlson experimented by making his own dried, salted fish with walleye and panfish and lots of kosher salt. He soaked the fillets for a day or two and created this recipe.

Jamie Carlson's Salt Fish Brandade

½ pound boiled potatoes

5 ounces rehydrated salt fish fillets

2 tablespoons unsalted butter

⅓ cup heavy cream

1 clove garlic (minced)

juice from half a lemon

2 sprigs fresh thyme

2 tablespoons olive oil

1. Simmer the salt fish fillets in water for 5 to 6 minutes, then remove fillets and bring the water back to a boil. Boil the potatoes until fork tender. While potatoes are boiling, pick over fish fillets for any bones.

2. When potatoes are done, drain them and mash them with a potato masher. Mix in remaining ingredients, including fish, and mash together until well incorporated. Taste; add salt if needed.

3. To serve, spoon brandade onto slices of crusty bread and garnish with minced shallots, lemon zest, and chives. Serves 4 as an appetizer; makes twenty-five hors d'oeuvres.

Strange Scandinavian Concoctions

From Fish Balls to Lutefisk Hotdish

Fishing as a means of survival was cemented into the consciousness of early explorers. A large mural at the Viking Inn in Viroqua, Wisconsin, depicts a Nordic fisherman with a big white beard returning home and being hugged by his kids. Even the Kensington Runestone, that mysterious rock that is supposedly evidence that Nordic explorers reached northern Minnesota in 1362, tells of "Eight Goths and twenty-two Norwegians . . . were to fish one day." But how did they cook the fish?

One of the more unusual fish recipes that likely resulted from these Norse berserkers out on a "viking," as they referred to their raids, was lutefisk. The legend says enemies burned the cod drying on birch racks, and a heavy rain doused the fire, leaving puddles of fish and birch ash (basically lye). When the starving Vikings returned, they tasted these fish puddles. After experiencing painful stomachaches, they learned to rinse out the lye "in fresh water to make fine food," according to *History of the Nordic Peoples,* written in 1555 by Olaus Magnus.

Lutefisk has a prominent place at the Scandinavian *julebord,* or Christmas table, but what other unusual seafood recipes might be at the "groaning table," as the fish-filled yuletide table is jokingly called? For starters, open-faced sandwiches (*smørbrød* in Norwegian or *smørrebrød* in Danish) of white bread topped with salmon or small shrimp or herring, which is sometimes curried with a very thin lemon slice on top. Eighty-proof aquavit accompanies this first course, and beer is added for the next.

One of the most popular warm dishes are white fish balls, *fiskeboller,* which are rivaled by the bigger *klubb* dumplings made from flour, grated potatoes, and ground fish boiled in fish-head broth. If that doesn't entice you, perhaps fish hotdish could fill your plate. The traditional tuna hotdish takes many different forms, such as tuna loaf custard. More adventurous eaters should try codfish casserole from *Original Scandinavian Recipes* or the surprisingly delicious lutefisk hotdish with freshly ground nutmeg.

These recipes often call for fish to be whipped for dishes like Swedish salt cod *kabiljo* pudding and *fiskegrøt* (fish porridge) using ground haddock (or other whitefish), thick cream, and cornstarch to bind

Keeping fish in drain cleaner, or lye, may sound extreme, but the caustic chemicals were easily rinsed and could preserve the fish for long periods of time. Here Mrs. Olsen prepares a lutefisk dinner at her house in St. Paul in 1936. PHOTOGRAPH BY *ST. PAUL DAILY NEWS.* COURTESY OF THE MINNESOTA HISTORICAL SOCIETY.

Scandinavians developed many variations on classic fish dishes, from herring soup to lutefisk hotdish. This photograph shows a classic Norwegian *julebord*, or Christmas table, filled with Scandinavian concoctions at the Viking Hotel in Oslo in 1953. COURTESY OF THE NATIONAL ARCHIVES OF NORWAY.

it all together. Fish mousse (or, more accurately, fish aspic), called *fiskekabaret*, makes a regular appearance at the *julebord* of the Mindekirken Norwegian Lutheran Church in Minneapolis.

Besides anchovy casserole and *sild suppe* (herring soup), one of the riskiest-sounding meals has a long tradition going all the way back to the founding fathers of the United States. Anglers slice the cheek

156

To a Scandinavian in 1956, this Christmas gift basket meant a joyous yuletide celebration. Imagine Santa's bag filled with fish balls, kippers, and smoked oysters . . . but what would the bad kids get? PHOTOGRAPH BY NORTON AND PEEL. COURTESY OF THE MINNESOTA HISTORICAL SOCIETY.

meat from freshwater fish for a small snack, just as children in Norwegian fishing villages carved the tastiest meat from around the jaws of giant cod to put tongues and cheeks on the holiday dinner table. Even Thomas Jefferson placed large orders for cod tongues to be delivered to his Monticello estate from the North Sea. The question remains, though: how did he cook them?

Any trip up Lake Superior's north shore in Minnesota requires a stop for fresh or smoked lake trout or whitefish. Lou's Fish House is a fishermen's favorite. PHOTOGRAPH BY THE AUTHOR.

Fish Shops

Guaranteed Limit!

"I get depressed when I look at the price per pound for walleye at the grocery store, as it's often under $15 per pound," wrote Robert Zink in *The Three-Minute Outdoorsman*. "I calculate what it costs me to catch them, figuring in the boat, gear, gas, and lodging. Somewhere near $11.7 million per pound is my estimate." At that point, sport fishers decide that store-bought fish isn't so bad after all.

In the early years of commercial fishing operations on the Great Lakes, massive amounts of catch were shipped to nearby cities and as far away as the East Coast and St. Louis. The lakes offered "inexhaustible" amounts of fish. In 1917, gill nets that could stretch up to two miles were used by 273 licensed commercial fisheries. Fishermen strung so many nets on Lake Superior that supposedly they could reach across the country from the Atlantic to the Pacific. Fishers stuffed 125 pounds of fresh fish into "herring boxes without topses" made from fresh poplar that wouldn't leave any flavor on the meat. Steamboats traveled the coasts twice a week and whistled their presence to fishing families. The fishermen rowed out to deliver their catch, often during the dark of night. When roads finally reached these remote spots, the fishermen simply left their fish on the side of the street to be picked up.

Fishing families then recognized that they could sell their goods directly to customers. Today, tourists make a point of stopping at Lou's Fish House in Two Harbors, Minnesota, or Susie-Q Fish Market in Two Rivers, Wisconsin, to stock the fridge with fresh or smoked fish. Perhaps the most famous retail fishmonger in Minnesota was Ed Morey of Motley. He sold Sunday newspapers and vegetables until he ran into a fisherman from Lake of the Woods who had a broken-down truck full of fish. He swapped vegetables for three boxes of fresh walleye, perch, and saugers. He was tricked, though: he thought the fisherman had sold him a couple of boxes of "catfish," but "I found out the darn catfish was burbot—eelpout!" he wrote in *Classic Minnesota Fishing Stories*. "If you want a guaranteed limit go to Morey's! Many a limit has been 'caught' at Morey's retail counters."

Another long-standing fish processor is Olsen's Fish Company in north Minneapolis, in operation since 1910. Chris Dorff took over the company from his father in 1994 and remembered the early days: "You used to be able to smell [Olsen's] a block away. The herring boxes, your clothes, they all smelled. The cardboard, wooden pallets. Some companies will only use plastic pallets now."

Brad Hanson, a friend of Dorff who used to work at Olsen's, told me, "I'd wear the same clothes every day because they were ruined. Now they're laundered every day."

Hanson recalled that even when he was wearing gloves, the vinegar and fish smell got into his pores. "This is the reason I finished college. A barrel rolled over me. I buckled my knee, and all the herring poured all over me." Dorff and Hanson laughed as they remembered past days at the fish company.

Despite their stories about the old days, the operation is now remarkably clean and odor-free. Dorff showed me a mini silo filled with vinegar shipped from Chicago and bags of sugar to make pickled herring. Because of the limited number of lake herring available, all fish come from the Atlantic already cut and salted. A specialty from the past was smoked

FISKESALG PAA BERGENS TORV. 99

The origins of local fish businesses on Lake Superior's north shore were open-air markets like this one in Bergen, Norway. COURTESY OF THE NATIONAL ARCHIVES OF NORWAY.

pickled herring, but demand dropped off. Dorff reports that now 80 percent of Olsen's operation is dedicated to pickled herring. Almost all the rest is lutefisk, making Olsen's one of the last fish businesses in the country to make this lye-soaked cod. The only other one in Minnesota is Day Fish Company

FISH FRIES AND FISH BOILS

in Braham, which began in 1968 in the town's old cooperative creamery and is open only from October 1 to January 31. Before the Christmas season, two semitrailers each deliver thirty thousand pounds of dried fish to Olsen's. "That's about a half million dollars on each truck," Dorff calculated, since it will sell

Ed Morey's business began by serendipity when a truck filled with fish from Lake of the Woods broke down in his town of Motley. He is pictured here, on the right, with Loren Morey on the left, smoking the day's recent catch. COURTESY OF MOREY'S SEAFOOD INTERNATIONAL; REPRINTED WITH PERMISSION.

Susie-Q Fish Market of Two Rivers, Wisconsin, is a classic neighborhood fishmonger located a half-block from West Twin River, which feeds into Lake Michigan. PHOTOGRAPH BY THE AUTHOR.

Now the largest processor of lutefisk in the world, Olsen's Fish Company has sold its products at grocery stores for decades. PHOTOGRAPH BY NORTON AND PEEL. COURTESY OF OLSEN'S FISH COMPANY.

Tins of fish on modern store shelves may be mostly limited to sardines and anchovies, but Olsen's Fish Company of north Minneapolis did brisk business with herring Snak-Paks, perfect for a picnic or a kid's lunch. PHOTOGRAPHS BY THE AUTHOR.

for twenty-two dollars per pound when reconstituted after the eleven- to twelve-day process of rinsing the caustic acid daily to lower the pH.

To expand lutefisk's market, "Dorff thinks younger people would take to lutefisk if only it were bacon-wrapped, or stuffed into tacos," according to the *Minneapolis Star Tribune* from Christmas Day 2014. The journalist returned to the newsroom to make "mac-and-cheese lutefisk," not suggested by Olsen's. As sales of lutefisk slipped, herring sales were rising. Olsen's recommends "roll-ups" of herring wrapped around a dill pickle.

Morey's emphasizes that two servings of fatty fish (such as herring) a week is recommended by the American Heart Association. If that doesn't convince skeptics, listen to President Herbert Hoover telling what to do when the fish aren't biting: "In the end you may catch the big one, but the average expense is about one thousand dollars per fish. You can get one of equal weight, although a little less flavor, at a market for less than five dollars."

Gorby Fever

"The Walleye That Saved the World"

The Berlin Wall fell in 1989, and thousands of East Germans entered West Berlin. Western Euro-

peans worried about a massive refugee crisis, but most just returned to their homes in the East in the evening once they knew they had free passage back and forth. As graffiti on the wall said, "They came, they saw, they did a little shopping." Suddenly the Cold War with the evil Communist empire came to an unexpected and much welcomed thaw.

Soviet leader Mikhail Gorbachev, the architect of the new openness called *glasnost*, visited Minnesota the following year with his wife Raisa and received a rock star's reception. After a four-day summit with President George H. W. Bush, the Gorbachevs flew in a Russian Aeroflot plane to Minneapolis and were driven in Soviet Zil limos to St. Paul, where the flag of

the USSR flew over the governor's mansion. Journalists quipped that Gorbachev was "the second-most powerful man in the world" but the most important at the moment since he almost single-handedly ended the threat of imminent atomic annihilation for the planet. "The spirited Soviet leader abandoned his limo a block early as thousands of pushy capitalists cheered in joyous confusion," wrote a student journalist at the *Minnesota Daily*.

"'Gorby' plunged into crowds to shake hands, American-style, several times during the day, including on Summit Avenue, where reporters said he was 'working the crowds like a politician on election eve,'" according to the *St. Paul Pioneer Press*. Vendors sold

Soviet premier Mikhail Gorbachev supped on fresh walleye pike at the Minnesota governor's mansion in 1990. Notice the state-shaped "birthmark" on his portrait that hangs near the bathrooms at the Tavern on Grand in St. Paul. COURTESY OF TAVERN ON GRAND.

joke Gorbachev/Mondale campaign buttons and warm T-shirts proclaiming in Russian and English: "Hugs to the kids in Russia from the kids in Minnesota." The admiration was mutual. Minnesota's First Lady Lola Perpich spent time with Raisa Gorbachev and said there is "a very warm and fuzzy feeling that the Soviets have of Minnesota."

The only problem was the menu. David Wildmo, owner of the Tavern on Grand in St. Paul, was not pleased that Governor Perpich planned to serve Wisconsin Provimi veal topped with Minnesota morel mushroom sauce. Gorbachev had even considered going to Murray's Steak House in Minneapolis. What about classic Minnesota walleye? Wildmo called the governor's office and offered to serve his famous walleye. Wildmo's delicious walleye recipe is originally from his childhood in Bemidji, Minnesota, where he ate walleye at local fish fries. When Wildmo asked for the delicious recipe (light, not greasy), they flatly refused but gave him a sample of the batter as consolation. He had the sample chemically analyzed and then added his own special spices. He originally bought his walleye from Red Lake but soon had to buy fish from Canada when commercial walleye netting in Minnesota essentially closed down.

The fish proved a success for the Soviet premier, and nuclear war was once again averted. The Tavern on Grand promoted the fateful visit with a portrait of Gorbachev that replaces the famous birthmark on his balding head with a Minnesota-shaped mark and the caption reads "Try the Walleye." The restaurant serves up to two thousand pounds of walleye a week and has expanded options beyond the classic walleye sandwich to blackened walleye, walleye salad,

After the fall of the Berlin Wall, Minnesota-made Karkov Vodka ran these giant advertisements that featured the usually smiling Mikhail Gorbachev. The billboards were removed before Gorbachev visited Minnesota in 1990. ASSOCIATED PRESS PHOTO / JIM MONE. COPYRIGHT AP IMAGES.

walleye BLT, walleye tacos, walleye cakes, walleye in spring rolls, walleye-on-a-stick—everything except chocolate-covered walleye. The Tavern's atmosphere is classic northwoods, even though the restaurant is on busy Grand Avenue in St. Paul. The knotty pine walls reinforce the cabin-like look, and some are painted with clever trompe l'oeil images. Deer antler chandeliers hang from the ceiling, and big fish bas-

reliefs decorate the walls next to advertising posters for "The Crowning of Miss Walleye." The wait staff sport black T-shirts with a white slogan on the back: "There's nothing more worthless than one beer. —A. Widmo." Even so, the bar features local rhubarb wine as the best complement to the walleye.

Many, including Widmo, applauded the leader of the "Evil Empire," as Ronald Reagan called the

Soviet Union, but others were wary. The Minnesota welcoming committee worried that the anti-alcohol crusader Gorbachev would see billboards advertising Karkov vodka around the state; they showed Gorbachev, with his birthmark on the wrong side of his head, holding a bottle of the vodka and proclaiming "The Party's Over." The billboards were removed before his visit. His portly successor, Boris Yeltsin, was well known not to refuse a glass of the good stuff. He visited Minnesota two years after Gorbachev did; he skipped the fish and went right for the Spam. A photograph at the Hormel plant in Austin shows a glassy-eyed Yeltsin with a rosy-red nose sheepishly holding a can of Spam—perhaps he was suffering from jet lag. He gave his brown sport coat to the plant manager at Hormel as a souvenir and later told a crowd, "At least I still have my pants." He should have stuck to the walleye.

Dan Falbo's Boundary Waters Walleye

The Tavern on Grand declined revealing its secret recipe for fried walleye, but Dan Falbo, who grew up on Minnesota's Iron Range, offered his delicious and simple recipe.

1 cup flour

1 beer (preferably Hamm's, but any beer will do)

1 teaspoon of salt, black pepper, and paprika (optional)

8 small fish fillets, preferably walleye, perch, or bluegill

oil (not olive oil, since it must have a high smoking point)

Mix flour, beer, salt, pepper, and paprika in a bowl. Rinse fish and pat dry with paper towels. Put a good inch of oil into a frying pan and turn the burner to high. Dunk the fillets into the batter and set into the hot oil. Beware of the oil splattering. Turn on the fans, open the windows, and be prepared to smell like fish. The oil should be hot enough that the fish doesn't stick to the pan. Cook for about five minutes or until lightly brown. Serve with lemon or tartar sauce as desired.

Manna from Heaven!
Beer Delivery by Drone

Beer and fishing have always gone together—at least that's what advertisers would like us to think. Not only did breweries such as Gettelman and Holiday from Wisconsin, and Bosch and Pfeiffer from Michigan, make beer cans that featured fish, but special lures and bobbers included beer logos as if fish couldn't resist either. Schmidt Beer from St. Paul ran its famous wildlife series of cans with twenty-one different designs (several of fish) that became a must-have during the beer-can collecting rage in the 1970s. Hooking into this trend, Jim Beam distillery produced special-edition fish decanters for its bourbon that essentially funded the founding of the Freshwater Fishing Hall of Fame in Hayward, Wisconsin.

Hamm's Brewery, across town from Schmidt, ran numerous humorous television advertisements

Refreshing as the Land of Sky Blue Waters

#292031 © PABST BREWING CO., MILWAUKEE, WI

Just as anglers are snagged by ads for suds, why wouldn't fish submit to a Schlitz? Once you're hooked, there's no going back! PHOTOGRAPH BY THE AUTHOR.

Without a care in the world, the Hamm's Bear often took to the shore in an effort to reel in that one elusive fish.

Preferred...*for mellow moments*

Matching the mood of your moments of leisure, Hamm's is a beer of rare smoothness and subtle mellowness.

This has been our custom for 82 years: to malt our own prize barley, reaped in the fertile fields close by, to use crystal-clear artesian water, to brew our beer with surpassing skill under the guidance of a brewmaster who carries on the tradition for Hamm quality established by his father and grandfather.

Hamm's is preferred by millions. Today it can be your preference, too . . . because we are expanding our brewery, which already is known as one of the largest in the nation.

For your mellow moments, you too will certainly prefer Hamm's—truly the smooth and mellow beer.

Hamm's

Smooth and Mellow Beer

Theo. Hamm Brewing Co., St. Paul 1, Minn.

Sitting in the bass boat or fly fishing for hours often requires coffee in the morning and beer in the evening. Breweries like Hamm's and Schlitz hailed the northwoods pastime by releasing special fishing-themed advertisements.

featuring a goofy cartoon bear slipping on ice or catching all the fish because, well, he drinks beer. (Back then advertising liquor with cartoon characters wasn't taboo.) "Fish not biting? Then let's cool it with another Hamm's!" One advertisement features a Gilligan-like sailor lounging on a rubber inner tube who whistles for more Hamm's. The silly bear aboard a mini steamer loaded with beer brings the thirsty fisherman a refill on the double.

In 2014, Lakemaid Beer, brewed under contract by Schell's in New Ulm, Minnesota, brought beer distribution to a new level. In hopes of luring

A successful day of fishing in rural Wisconsin ends with a heavy stringer of fish, supper for a week. It's time to celebrate with a picnic of sandwiches and beer. MICHAEL J. PECOSKY COLLECTION.

Photo by
Geo. O. B. Gruetzmacher
Merrill Wis.

thirsty fishing fans, the clever company named the beer a "fisherman's lager" and featured a fishing game printed inside the bottle caps—imbibers need to collect many to play! Most notable, for publicity's sake, was the delivery of this fishermen's beverage via drone. A video uploaded to YouTube with no talking shows a phone ringing and someone answering and then scribbling coordinates for a GPS. A six-bladed drone is attached to a twelve-pack of "frosty winter lager" and the automatic little helicopter flies into the chilly air over a frozen Lake Waconia covered with ice shacks housing thirsty fishers. The intoxicating package arrives at the door of the savvy anglers who know where to get the good stuff.

Then the Feds stepped in. A federal judge declared that drones are no different from model airplanes, which have no strict regulations. The Federal Aviation Administration immediately appealed the

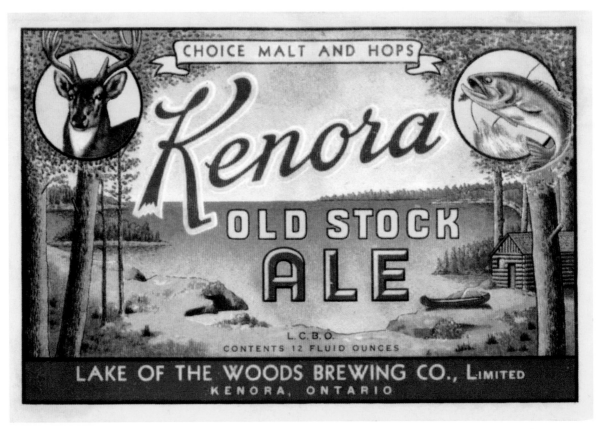

On both sides of the northern border, images of the bucolic north woods were popular for promoting and selling beer.

decision, which put drone beer delivery to parched anglers on hold. An astute writer at the *St. Paul Pioneer Press* pointed out on March 6, 2014, "The twelve-pack of beer in the video was not filled with bottles. Few drones available commercially have the power to move that much weight." Perhaps by the time the FAA allows beer from heaven, higher-powered drones will be able to pull their weight.

The Feds putting the kibosh on drinking in the north woods is nothing new. During Prohibition, Chicago gangsters retreated to cabins in Minnesota and Wisconsin to go "fishing." Al Capone had his retreat in Couderay, Wisconsin. Gangster Tommy Banks escaped the heat in the city at West Bearskin Lake, convenient for fishing expeditions and close enough to the Canadian border to haul in moonshine. Birchdale Villas on Lake Whitefish was a drop-off point for booze. On the north side of that big lake between Emily and Outing, a famous gangster (likely Baby Face Nelson) had a hideout. Automobiles, fishing skiffs, or mail boats delivered a stash of liquor hidden beneath bags of letters or fishing tackle down "the Old Whiskey Road" (County Road 145) to Birchdale Villas.

Lakemaid Beer dreams of delivery by drones; gangsters employed small planes that flew from Canada and dropped their hooch, surrounded by buoys, into the lake outside the lodges of Manhattan Beach in Crosslake or Breezy Point Hotel on Pelican Lake. "Fishermen" rowed out and brought in the catch of the day for northwoods shindigs. "Supposedly there were escape tunnels all over in case the police busted up the fun," the receptionist at the Pequot Lakes Chamber of Commerce told me. The

Breezy Point Hotel mysteriously burned down . . . did the cops feel humiliated that they never nabbed these miscreants? More likely the fire was an accident.

Before Prohibition made these clandestine booze runs necessary, even Minnesota's first territorial governor, Alexander Ramsey, brought a flask of the good stuff to enliven a fishing trip in 1852. According to *Once upon a Lake*, the gubernatorial fishing entourage forgot salt to flavor the fish. "It was the governor who suggested that brandy did just as well and who took the flask from the medicine chest. They all agreed that the dram made a piquant sauce." The inebriating influence surely made the fish more flavorful, and the tales of the one that got away became even more dramatic. 🐟

Throughout the north woods, mammoth fish dot the landscape. This trio, on display at the Freshwater Fishing Hall of Fame in Hayward, Wisconsin, creates the ultimate tourist attraction. PHOTOGRAPH BY THE AUTHOR.

CHAPTER SIX

The Art of the Fish

Monuments and Mammoths of the Deep

I only make movies to finance my fishing.

—*actor Lee Marvin*

On the windswept plains in the shadow of the enormous Wally the Walleye statue, Garrison, North Dakota, houses the state fishing hall of fame as a tribute to Dakotan bravado. Other fishing museums tout their lineup of classic outboard motors for trolling through weedy waters. The ultimate colossus of the deep is at the Freshwater Fishing Hall of Fame in Hayward, Wisconsin. Measuring 145 feet, a half-block long, this leaping fiberglass muskie was gutted to make a museum. Outside the belly of this whale is the "Sea of Fishes" with fiberglass statues of a variety of fish. Apart from looking like the perfect venue for a putt-putt golf tournament, the museum charts freshwater fishing records across the world.

Fish-Inspired Art

Fins, Scales, and Sharks

Images of fish date back to the earliest human petroglyph cave drawings. In early Finland, rather than drawing fish, musicians "played" them. The Finnish national epic, the *Kalevala*, tells of a fish-bone harp (the *kantele*) that the valiant protaganist Väinämöinen crafted from the bones of a pike with strings plucked from the heads of fair Finnish maidens who gave them willingly to the handsome young hero of the saga.

Canadian architect Frank Gehry became obsessed with the graceful curves of fish covered with sharp scales. Along with his wavy buildings covered with sheets of shimmering stainless steel in Bilbao, Los Angeles, and Minneapolis, he constructed a towering twenty-foot *Standing Glass Fish* from hundreds of razor-sharp panes of cut glass held with clear epoxy.

Swedish sculptor Carl Milles made a fish-themed fountain in St. Louis, *Wedding of Waters*, to honor the convergence of the Missouri and Mississippi rivers. The Scandinavian aesthetic was far too risqué for local alderman Hubert Hoeflinger, who complained in 1938: "I've been to a lot of weddings but I never saw one where everybody was naked. . . . Look at that lady trying to forward pass a fish. Look at that fellow with the corkscrews coming out of his head and a fish in his mouth. If those things are beautiful, then I'm crazy."

General Motors design visionary Harley Earl took fish fins and plopped them on avant-garde prototypes in the 1940s. After visiting the Selfridge Air Force Base in 1941 to see the P-38 fighter planes and the Douglas F-4D Skyray, Earl sketched his vision of the future but left off the wings and instead made ever-larger fins on his vehicles beginning with the 1948 Cadillac. The fins were openly ridiculed, but the bold new design was copied by nearly every other car manufacturer. The pinnacle of fish-like four-wheelers was Earl's 1956 Firebird II prototype, which was shaped like a shark with a gas turbine engine and titanium bodywork that wouldn't corrode from salt and water—just like sharkskin. The artistic designers envisioned that the Firebird II would emit an electronic beam to make contact with a control tower via its dashboard television screen, which would lead the car on a metallic strip down the "Safety Highway of the Future," an idea only realized today with driverless cars.

The year before, Citroën released its DS. Adoring Italian auto enthusiasts raved about it swimming through the streets and nicknamed it *lo squalo*, the shark, or the less flattering *il ferro da stiro*, the clothes iron. The idea of a shark car inspired automobile artist Tom Kennedy to make his one-of-a-kind *Ripper the Friendly Shark* art car with gills for air intakes and a single menacing dorsal fin. Fishy art cars have been covered with tanned salmon skin to make the vehicle waterproof and weather resistant, similar to Earl's titanium version. Other mechanical fish out of water are *Sashimi Tabernacle Choir*, created by Richard Carter and John Schroetoer, covered with dozens of Big Mouth Billy Bass plastered on a Volvo that sing Handel's "Hallelujah" chorus to spectators.

Even fish houses have inspired artists to produce a frozen version of Nevada's Burning Man festival. Alongside "Art Cars on Ice" events devised by artist Jan Elftmann and Macalester professor Ruthann

Architect Frank O. Gehry created this stunning *Standing Glass Fish* sculpture, which was housed first in the lobby of the Walker Art Center and then in the greenhouse of the Minneapolis Sculpture Garden. PHOTOGRAPH BY AUTHOR.

The most notable styling cue of the 1950s on overly long American automobiles was the fins, earning them the moniker "land sharks." GM designer Harley Earl's 1958 Firebird I, II, and III prototypes were conceived with tails, dorsal fins, and even "gills" that doubled as air intakes. PHOTOGRAPH COURTESY OF GENERAL MOTORS.

Tom Kennedy manufactured his *Ripper the Friendly Shark* art car as part of a long tradition of automotive designers looking to sleek creatures of the deep for inspiration. PHOTOGRAPH COPYRIGHT HARROD BLANK / WWW.ARTCARAGENCY.COM.

Godollei, and given the relatively few rules required to build a fish house, Art Shanty Projects features artist-designed icehouses on a Minnesota lake, most with a hole drilled in the ice for fishing. From giant robot-shaped icehouses to *DICEHOUSES,* five red dice rolling like a Yahtzee game, the artistic ice shanties compete with Aitkin's Fish House Parade for originality.

Turning a frozen lake into an art gallery may leave some scratching their heads, but fish have inspired many other even more outrageous art forms. As comedian Steven Wright said, "Last year I went fishing with Salvador Dalí. He was using a dotted line. He caught every other fish." Artist Seth Weiner designed the Terranaut II, a three-wheeled bicycle guided by the movements of a skittish goldfish in a fishbowl mounted on the self-propelled vehicle. As the fish moves, the three-wheeler goes in the same

Seth Weiner created *Terranaut II* to give this aquatic creature wheels to move about on land. Arguably the worst driver ever, the goldfish inside the fishbowl makes decisions about where to drive as a computer monitors its movements and steers the vehicle accordingly. PHOTOGRAPH COURTESY OF SETH WEINER.

Artist Gary Greff dreamed of luring motorists off Interstate 94 to his *Enchanted Highway* south of Regent, North Dakota, by creating eleven giant statues, including the whimsical *Fisherman's Dream* pictured here. PHOTOGRAPH COURTESY OF GARY GREFF, WWW.ENCHANTEDHIGHWAYND.COM.

random direction. This plays on the idea that human drivers are stuck in a fishbowl—or, as cultural critic Judith Hoos Fox suggested in *Inside Cars*, "In our cars we become goldfish: protected, unaware, disengaged." I hope we don't circle around like a driving goldfish.

Some towns try to lure visitors with fish art. Fort Atkinson, Wisconsin, has a metal catfish sculpture wedged downtown between two buildings over "Catfish Alley," where revelers gather for food and drink. Sculptor Gary Greff staged a massive project on the prairie of central North Dakota to bring visitors off the interstate into the town of Regent. As part of *Enchanted Highway*, Greff erected *Fisherman's Dream*, which re-creates the bottom of a lake with seaweed growing skyward amid giant northern pike, bass, and rainbow trout as if the water's surface is somewhere overhead in the clouds.

Cities may use fish art as a beautification project. Green Bay, Wisconsin, took an unsightly pedestrian underpass and transformed it into an "interactive immersion" tunnel. Motion sensors trigger a kaleidoscope of LED lights inside twenty-two luminous fish as though they had munched on radioactive promethium to give the otherwise drab passageway the feel of a Euro discotheque. Newaygo, Wisconsin, chose a more bucolic scene to beautify its Riverside Park. Cement fish heads protrude from a grassy field next to the Muskegon River as if they could snatch visitors' shoes for lunch.

Two cities followed the lead of many others in making multiple fiberglass statues and commissioning local artists to add the aesthetics. Walkerton, Ontario, features eleven sunfish-like sculptures

and placed them out of water around town. Detroit Lakes, Minnesota, upped the ante to thirty sunfish for its community art project; one is gussied up as a Viking fish to celebrate the predominant local heritage. To catch these giant sunnies, the town boasts a twenty-five-foot found-object fishing pole. The line is an old water-skiing rope; the eyes are basketball hoops; a giant wire spool is the reel, with old hockey sticks making up the crank. On this sculpture, even an ordinary leaning telephone pole becomes a fishing rod in the eye of an angler.

The Freshwater Fishing Hall of Fame

Into the Mouth of the Muskie

How do you ship a 145-foot muskie from Sparta, Wisconsin, to Hayward? Jerry Vettrus of Fiberglass Animals, Shapes, and Trademarks (FAST Corporation) recalls a huge traffic jam in 1979 when he brought the giant fish to the new Freshwater Fishing Hall of Fame. "The fish never would have fit on one truck, so we had to ship it to Hayward in parts and assemble it there. I don't think we'll ever do anything like that again, and I'm sure nobody could afford it now!" FAST made the fish in nine months and during the same year built the 55½-foot Jolly Green Giant statue for Blue Earth, Minnesota.

Hayward's five-hundred-ton fish is the largest fiberglass structure in the world—the mouth holds twenty people. Coupling a love of fishing with holy matrimony, six inspired couples have tied the knot in

An imposing
duo greets
visitors to the
Freshwater
Fishing Hall
of Fame in
Hayward,
Wisconsin.
PHOTOGRAPH BY
THE AUTHOR.

Inside the Freshwater Fishing Hall of Fame Museum, those fish hiding beneath the waves are brought into the light and stuffed for all to see. COLLECTION OF SWELLMAP.

Yes, son, we finally caught the big one! The playful outdoor exhibits in Hayward have brought generations of anglers together for decades. PHOTOGRAPHS COURTESY OF JACOB KREJCI.

the muskie's mouth. Outside the belly of this whale is the "Sea of Fishes," an entire stringer of underwater creatures vying for attention. Any of the other fish statues—a fiberglass walleye, Coho salmon, bluegill, perch, smallmouth bass, rainbow trout—would make an angler proud, but these seem like bait compared to the walk-through muskie. Entering the innards of the fish like Jonah or Geppetto, one is greeted by the "World's Largest Nightcrawler" hung on the wall.

If that's not enough, another building (which isn't remotely fish-shaped) houses more than 350 classic outboard motors, six thousand lures, and many rods and reels. "We have more than one hundred thousand artifacts on seven acres," executive director Emmett Brown told me. The walls are decked with grip-and-grin photographs of record-setting freshwater fishermen from around the world holding their trophy fish.

The hall of fame began when "Robert Kutz had a dream and asked several local business owners to help him get a start through the '60s," according to Brown. In the early '70s, Kutz recruited the assistance of the Jim Beam distillery, based in Chicago. Beam donated all profits from twelve collectible fish decanters from 1971 to 1983 to help start the museum, which was "enough revenue to build the entrance building and the Muskie. In 1982 the main museum was opened, and the lion's share of it came from royalties," Brown said. It began "as really more or less a way to push tourism here in Hayward. We've grown far beyond that and have become a regular stopping ground for the governors of Wisconsin. Denny Green was here a couple of summers ago. We've inducted many celebrities; you don't have to catch a big fish to get in." But it sure doesn't hurt if you reel in a giant muskie.

Chin-Whiskered Charlie

A Muskie Hoax?

As the king of freshwater fish, the muskie is the most sought after by freshwater sport fishers, and whoever catches the biggest becomes legend. No wonder controversy haunts the record holders. In 2005, arguments escalated when the trophy fish caught by confirmed world record holder Louie Spray came under scrutiny. Forensics specialist Dan Mills from

WESTWOODS RESORT
NEVIS, MINN.

WESTWOODS RESORT
NEVIS, MINN.

ON LAKE BELLE TAIN

The HOME *of the* TIGER MUSKIE!

Playing a good-natured, sometimes contentious rivalry, both Wisconsin and Minnesota lay claims to being the true "Home of the Muskie." *OPPOSITE:* COURTESY OF THE WISCONSIN HISTORICAL SOCIETY, WHI-79611. *ABOVE:* SUMMERS PAST IN PARK RAPIDS.

Louie Spray also caught this world-record muskie, in 1939, near Hayward, Wisconsin. PHOTOGRAPH BY ALLAN BORN. COURTESY OF THE WISCONSIN HISTORICAL SOCIETY, WHI-96787.

Toronto did a "photogrammetric" analysis of the alleged sixty-nine-pound muskie, nicknamed "Chin-Whiskered Charlie," caught by Spray. "Accusations of rank jealousy and anti-Wisconsin intrigue have been hurled at the Illinois-based World Record Muskie Alliance, which sponsored the scientific study of the fish Mr. Spray landed in 1949," according to *Ottawa Citizen* in a 2005 article, "Something Smells Fishy about World-Record Muskie."

"Skepticism has surrounded Mr. Spray's claim for decades," the article said. "But ten years ago—after an alleged 69-pound, 15-ounce muskie caught by New Yorker Art Lawton on the St. Lawrence River in 1957 was ruled a hoax—Mr. Spray and Chin-Whiskered Charlie took their place as Number 1 in the world." After that, new investigations looked into Spray's claim since some deemed the fish too skinny to weigh so much. Others speculated that he filled the fish with wet sand to increase the weight because if he had the world record, he would be much sought after as a guide. To make matters worse, Spray's stuffed fish burned in a fire.

As a forensics specialist, Mills typically used computer and physics technology to examine crime scenes—figuring bullet trajectory, extrapolating criminals' heights from grainy video, reconstructing traffic accidents—but this was the first time he had examined a fish in a photograph. He ruled that the muskellunge was only fifty-five inches long, not Spray's claim of sixty-three inches, and the claimed

Championship fish always make a good photo opportunity. Here, Wayne King *(left)* looks over a Minnesota muskie caught by Arthur F. Bratrud of Minneapolis, mid-1940s. PHOTOGRAPH BY BRUCE STIFFORD STUDIO, HENNEPIN COUNTY LIBRARY, MINNEAPOLIS PHOTO COLLECTION.

girth of 31.25 inches was also much too large. Some claimed that the taxidermist added several inches to the stuffed muskie. The World Record Muskie Alliance called Spray's fish "a fraud of historic proportions" and asked the Freshwater Fishing Hall of Fame in Hayward to reconsider.

Cynics wondered if this could be a turf battle between the Wisconsin-based hall of fame and the Illinois-based alliance. Others speculated that the Canadians started this cross-border feud by hiring the Toronto-based scientist because a Canadian caught a sixty-five-pound muskie in 1988 in Georgian Bay's Blackstone Harbour, which is currently third in line for the world record. If Spray's claim is disqualified, the new world record would be a 67-pound, 8-ounce muskie caught by Wisconsin fisherman Cal Johnson a few months before Spray caught his, which the International Game Fish Association in Florida recognizes as the world record muskie. That fish is stuffed and displayed at the Moccasin Bar a couple of blocks from the hall of fame in Hayward. Now the Canadian forensics specialist has been asked to review Johnson's fish as well.

"We know that adding Spray's patently false muskellunge records to the already long list of 'Muskie Crimes of the Century' represents yet another historic disillusionment for the entire muskellunge community," states a synopsis by the World Record Muskie Alliance. The Freshwater Fishing Hall of Fame dutifully examined the claims, weighed the evidence, interviewed witnesses of Spray's catch at Chippewa Flowage in Wisconsin, and stood by Spray's record. Despite the evidence presented by the World Record Muskie Alliance and the Canadian forensics expert, the Hall of Fame released a document that declared, "The fact remains that Louie Spray's 1949 world record muskie is exceptionally well documented and the NFWFHF is confident that the fish was as big as claimed."

Larry Ramsell, a volunteer world records adviser and fish historian for the Hall of Fame, resigned in protest when Spray's claim was not rejected because of the new evidence. The Bloomington, Illinois, newspaper *Pantagraph* reported on September 27, 2007, that Ramsell said that they just desired to keep the prize for the largest muskie in Hayward "to pump life into the town's lagging economy." Ramsell took matters into his own hands by completing a 1,366-page, two-volume *Compendium of Muskie Angling History*. He devotes nearly a quarter of the space of the first volume to arguing for the reinstatement of the 69-pound, 15-ounce muskie caught in New York by Art Lawton in 1957 that was discredited.

Executive director of the Hall of Fame, Emmett Brown, defended the decisions of the board. "Everyone's entitled to their opinion," he told the *Wisconsin State Journal*. "The Louis Spray record doesn't exist due to bias of the Hall or its board. It stands on its own merit." Strangely, the *Journal* reported, "Ramsell takes issue with revisionist history spurred by modern scientific attempts to analyze photographic evidence. He says muskellunge fishing history should be left alone. 'We can't prove (or disprove records) one way or the other. . . . I call them historic."

As a result, a new group with a lengthy name and long acronym, the International Committee of the Modern Day Muskellunge World Record Program (MDMWRP), was established to verify fish within the fifty-eight to sixty-eight pound range, which is considered the most this species can weigh. The current champion, Joseph Seeberger, landed a fifty-eight-pound muskie on Lake Bellaire in Michigan.

Has anyone mentioned the supposed 70-pound, 4-ounce muskie caught by Bob Malo on display at the Dun Rovin Lodge just outside Hayward?

Bena's Big Muskie

Red Eyes from Coca-Cola

Halfway between Bemidji and Grand Rapids on Highway 2 in northern Minnesota, a sixty-five-foot fish with a gaping mouth stands as the ultimate stuffed prize for fishers who come back empty-handed from nearby Lake Winnibigoshish. If you can't catch it, build it! In the spirit of the old trick photo postcards, "One day these two spearfishermen stop in and want to know if they can use a ladder to climb up on top of the fish for a photo!" Rita Wichmann told me in 1999, when she was owner of the Big Fish in Bena. "Enough is enough!" she told them.

A large sign implores visitors: "Please Don't Steal the Teeth!" "All these people stop by to take their picture with the fish and want to take something home with them," Wichmann complained, "so they take the teeth as souvenirs. I suppose we really should sell T-shirts." Back then, she wanted to sell it and retire. "What can I say good about it?" she says. "It's a pain, not a moneymaker." Regardless, Bena's Big Fish has become a landmark that has appeared in numerous magazines and at the beginning of *National Lampoon's Vacation* with Chevy Chase.

The Big Fish was born in the summer of 1958. Local Butch Dahl worked at the gas station in town—a red, white, and blue pagoda. It is a strange sight on the Leech Lake Indian Reservation, where one would expect to see log cabins, teepees, or wigwams. "My grandfather made this gas station," Dahl said. He employed his inherited skills to construct the biggest fish in the state. He told me how all the other towns had drive-in restaurants, but Bena couldn't compete. Dahl remembers, "We took 1 by 4s, soaked 'em in water, and bent 'em for the ribs." The fish's curved frame reaches fourteen feet into the air. "We nailed sheets of tar paper over the ribs and slapped on a coat of paint." After the long teeth were carved, "We needed some eyes. We looked around and found a couple of Coca-Cola signs." The round red Coke signs still stare at the highway.

The Big Fish was open for just a couple of years as a drive-in with a little take-out window on the side. For a while, tourists could walk into its mouth to buy souvenirs, but tar paper isn't made to last northern Minnesota winters. "We have to paint it almost every year, you know," Wichmann said.

In May 2009, the Minnesota Preservation Alliance listed the muskie as one of the endangered sites in the state. Paul Reimer, who owns the adjacent Big Fish Supper Club, watched the fish slowly decline but couldn't afford to fix it up. Gary Kirt of Medina stepped in to save the day when he heard about the fish's imminent demise. Kirt grew up in the area and wanted to give something back. "I remember throwing frogs at semis on Highway 2 when I was a kid, and I've driven by the Big Fish frequently over the years," he told *Minneapolis Star Tribune* reporter

Bena, Minnesota, wanted a drive-through restaurant, but the big hamburger franchises deemed the town far too small. Locals came together to construct their own, with a window on the left where customers could place their order. PHOTOGRAPH BY THE AUTHOR.

The vast assortment of fish and state-of-the-art exhibitions mesmerize visitors at the Great Lakes Aquarium in Duluth, Minnesota. PHOTOGRAPH BY THE AUTHOR.

Curt Brown in an article published on September 12, 2009. Thanks to the attention, Bena's big muskie should last another fifty years, but it will likely still need touch-up paint each summer.

The Great Lakes Aquarium

Behold the Cuddly Sturgeon!

When the doors open at 10 a.m., children storm in and want the fish to react. Many of the exhibits encourage visitors to help conserve our precious lakes and rivers, but kids want to push and pull. Signs beg them not to tap on the glass, not to use flash cameras, not to put their hands in the water, and not to throw anything into the water. Not surprisingly, muskies and northern pike are kept out of reach, since little fingers might become a scrumptious snack.

Hanging from the ceiling above the ticket counter is a giant burbot, or eelpout, which looks surprisingly graceful despite most anglers' dread of this slippery freshwater cod. This is just a hint of what lies ahead, including giant two-story fish tanks and an otter display sure to please the wee ones.

Compared to the kaleidoscope of colors of saltwater fish, freshwater fish are relatively lackluster; they are generally shades of dull green with a little yellow or red perhaps. To keep the crowd interested, a display on Mediterranean fish shows creepy manta rays. Another exhibit features colorful clown fish from the South Pacific schooling around a mock shipwreck, and a black light illuminates elegant jellyfish swooshing through the waves. The highlight for little visitors is two scuba divers who plunge into the big pool to feed hungry fish and nearly get their fingers nibbled. The prehistoric-looking sturgeons are especially affectionate, and divers pet them as they gobble herring in their bizarre mouths under their snouts. Kids can't resist this love fest and rub against the aquarium glass from outside.

A Family Affair

Commercial Fishing Museums

"The red fish house was the center of activity for the small community," said Ted Tofte. He lent his last name to the village on the north shore of Lake Superior that now houses the North Shore Commercial Fishing Museum. Up and down the coast, dozens of Scandinavian fishing families, such as the Toftes, Fenstads, Sves, Crofts, and Jacobsens, revived a fishing industry that had been practically abandoned when the American Fur Company declared bankruptcy in 1842 and gave up its fishing operations.

Arriving with fishing skills, these Scandinavians set to work, lugging in fish to fill their little boats up to the gunwales. Some skiffs had a pointed bow and stern and could be rowed in either direction; the famous Mackinaws were double-ended sailboats that could be rowed as well. To save energy and go farther into the lake, car engines were eventually rigged up as outboard motors on a skiff. With the onset of winter, most European fishers weren't accustomed to ice fishing but soon adapted; the catch was primarily for their own consumption to survive the cold months.

When fishermen came in from the big lake during the summer, the entire family was put to work.

As the tourist trade and recreational fishing slowly overtook commercial fishing operations on Lake Superior, the North Shore Commercial Fishing Museum sought to preserve the history of the industry. PHOTOGRAPH BY THE AUTHOR.

George Hanson's fishing business in Two Harbors, Minnesota, was one of the most prosperous on the north shore when this photograph was taken in 1910. COURTESY OF THE MINNESOTA HISTORICAL SOCIETY.

Herring boxes galore! A testament to the seemingly endless schools of fish in Lake Superior around 1916 is displayed in Two Harbors. PHOTOGRAPH BY WILLIAM F. ROLEFF. COURTESY OF THE MINNESOTA HISTORICAL SOCIETY.

Women usually stayed on shore cleaning, smoking, and selling fish. According to the Wisconsin Maritime Museum in Manitowoc, "Fishermen built their own boats while women and children knitted nets." Near Manitowoc, at Two Rivers, Wisconsin, "a majority of the women and children spend most of the winter making nets for local supply and for shipment to other fishing towns," the U.S. Commission of Fish and Fisheries stated in 1887.

Early nets were made of linen or heavy cotton; they had to be dried or they would rot. To preserve the material, families dunked nets in boiling linseed oil, which was highly combustible. Rather than dangling nets from balconies to dry, they used large revolving net reels to store and dry nets that were hundreds of feet long. Eventually, old corks and sinkers that had been used on nets were replaced with colorful plastic buoys, and blue vitriol (copper sulfate) replaced the flammable linseed oil. Now, thanks to modern monofilament line, fishing families no longer spend long winter months stitching nets.

The museum in Manitowoc describes in detail the difficult times of these commercial fishermen. "A 1984 Coast Guard study showed that commercial fishing was the nation's deadliest profession, with a death rate seven times the national average for other industries," according to one display. Another quotes Wisconsin fisherman Tim Weborg about why he chose this work if it's so dangerous: "Once you get started you can't stop. The family . . . we go back three generations in commercial fishing. It's like father and son. It gets in your blood." An early report from 1895 by the Wisconsin Commissioners of Fisheries confirms the museum's claims: "The lives of lake fishermen are not easy ones . . . oil skins sheeted with ice, numb fingers cut and bleeding from drawing in freezing nets, and faces frost bitten by icy spray are common experiences." The payoff for this perilous profession was that, given the long hours, fishermen could earn a bit more than the national average. Industrial workers in the United States earned an average of four hundred dollars per year in 1892, while an independent fisherman could make thirty dollars more than that. A salaried fisherman would haul in just two hundred dollars. The advantage of being a self-employed fisherman kept pace through the 1970s.

The North Shore Commercial Fishing Museum chronicles the downfall of the fishing industry on Lake Superior in the 1960s due to waste rock from the taconite processing plant at Silver Bay. The Reserve Mining Company dumped thousands of pounds of fine rock into the lake, which stirred up the crystalline water, and the fish population plummeted. Writer and fisherman Jim Harrison didn't mince words when talking about such contaminators: "I am privately in favor of the death penalty for any form of pollution not speedily rectified. If you are keen on trout fishing, I advise that you log thousands of hours a summer, because the signs, short of radical ecological surgery, point to its demise." Finally, in the 1970s, the EPA investigated. Judge Miles Lord ordered the dumping of waste into the lake to stop, effective immediately—the first time in the history of the country that a large industrial operation was shut down to protect the environment. Slowly, herring and trout have made a comeback.

These museums demonstrate the tension between commercial and recreation fishing and the move away from large-scale fishing operations. "It is a global trend to move away from commercial fishing," University of Minnesota fisheries professor Peter Sorensen told me. "A recreational fisherman gets a hotel, pays for gas, buys a twenty-five-thousand-dollar boat, so it's probably a thousand or at least a hundred dollars per fish caught. A commercial fisherman gets about seventy-five cents a pound." In the end, many anglers may stop at the fish market for dinner.

Fish Sculptures

Into the Belly of the Beast

"The one that got away," "the lunker to end all lunkers"—exaggeration is part of the obsession with fishing. Towns near lakes have boldly claimed all kinds of superlatives, with many declaring themselves the "Capital of the World" of a certain delicious fish. Edwardsburg, Michigan, calls itself the "Live Bait Capital of the World"—does this really attract tourists?

Hand-colored postcards dating back to the 1920s feature fishermen riding enormous rainbow trout and other creatures of the deep with the caption "The Fish Are Hungry Here!" The monsters gobble the poor boaters like bait. Were these cards sent as a warning to gullible city slickers to keep them from venturing north to eat all the fish or to lure them to catch the big one? Perhaps these goofy postcards were the muse that inspired industrious towns to erect enormous fiberglass fish on Main Street. These piscatorial icons spread the good word to passing tourists and let them dream of landing the levia-

than of a lifetime. Huge fish sculptures make perfect photo opportunities to portray modern versions of *The Old Man and the Sea*—visitors return home with a photograph instead of bones and exaggeration.

SUNNIES

Starting with sunfish, little Orr, Minnesota, has a colorful bluegill attached to the town's welcome sign. Fishtale Bar and Grill of New Prague, Minnesota, hoisted a giant sunfish high on a light-up sign to entice eaters but inexplicably offers only walleye as a fishy entrée. Wisconsin wins the battle of the bluegills since Birchwood boasts a fourteen-foot sunfish sculpture along Highway 48 to welcome visitors to the "Bluegill Capital of Wisconsin." Not to be outdone, Onalaska, Wisconsin, almost doubled the size of that fish in 1998 with the twenty-five-foot "Sunny the Sunfish" along Highway 35 that was named for Mayor Clarence "Sunny" Stellner. Political hoodlums took revenge and spray painted the helpless fish, who was then lovingly repainted by residents of the "Sunfish Capital of the World."

WHISKERED FISH

In a class by itself is the "World's Largest Bullhead" in Crystal Lake, Iowa. Measuring a respectable twelve feet, this smiling bullhead has no competition, since no other town wants to promote bullheads swimming in its waters.

The bullhead's big cousin, the catfish, has a lot of contenders. The most joyous catfish has to be the yellow and blue smiling "Chuck the Channel Cat," erected in 1986 in Selkirk, Manitoba, to promote the town as "Catfish Capital of the World." Not so fast!

Near the Canadian border, Orr, Minnesota, erected this happy bluegill as part advertising and part fish statue. PHOTOGRAPH BY THE AUTHOR.

Floodwood, Minnesota, claims the same title and has its three-day Catfish Days festival to prove it. The only statue in town, though, is a measly six-foot blue catfish carved from wood. Even the small town of Trempealeau, Wisconsin, on the Mississippi River boasts a nineteen-foot catfish statue for its Catfish Days in July.

Although Franklin, Minnesota, may not have a giant statue, as the "Catfish Capital of Minnesota" the town sponsors the romantic Kiss a Catfish Contest with revolted contestants sporting disgusted scowls when cuddling with a catfish. Smooching a flathead may seem harmless, but a mother in Arkansas held up a mudcat to tease her thirteen-year-old boy with some loving. KATV from Little Rock reported on June 19, 2013, that one of the barbs from the wiggling

In Wahpeton, North Dakota, Wahpper, the "World's Largest Catfish," watches over fellow mudcats swimming in the stream. A couple of his whiskers were broken off, and now a dainty metal fence encloses the five-thousand-pound fish. PHOTOGRAPH BY THE AUTHOR.

fish's fins impaled the boy's neck near his carotid artery. He was airlifted to a hospital, where doctors carefully removed the spine. The terrified boy was fine and the fish was delicious.

Despite the dangerous barbs, one of the main producers of farm-raised catfish, Belzoni, Mississippi, declared itself "Catfish Capital of the World." To prove the point, a forty-foot "King Cat" sculpture is stuck in the muck of a pond as a lively fountain shoots water through the beast's head like a whale's blowhole. Purists may question whether this hollow beast with a body of chicken wire can enter into the competition of catfish statues. Although the statue is not comely, an adjacent catfish museum compensates for the artist's lack of creativity (or laziness). An equally large but more impressive catfish guards

Minnesota governor Luther Youngdahl paid tribute to what was then the "World's Largest Tiger Muskie" at its inauguration in 1950 in Nevis, Minnesota. Despite the warning in the fish's mouth to "Keep Out," who can resist the photo op?
PHOTOGRAPH BY THE AUTHOR.

the banks of the Red River of the North in Wahpeton, North Dakota. Made by Dave Oswald of Sparta, Wisconsin, Wahpper the catfish ties Mississippi's King Cat at forty feet, but as of 2009 the prize for the world's largest catfish goes to the impressive fifty-foot Muddy the Mudcat in Dunnville, Ontario, who reigns over the town's Mudcat Festival in June.

MONSTROUS MUSKIES

Muskies are one of the largest fish in freshwater lakes and the perfect prize for any self-respecting angler, so muskie statues are the largest, and even small ones are big. To this day, picnickers can't resist staging photographs of being swallowed by the "World's Largest Tiger Muskie" in Nevis, Minnesota—at least this is what the town claimed when the 30½-foot fish was cemented in place in 1950. This claim was soon eclipsed by the sixty-five-foot muskellunge in Bena, Minnesota, that doubled as a drive-in restaurant.

The biggest fish in all of Canada leaps from the ground of Kenora, Ontario. Husky the Muskie looks to be bounding forty feet into the air. Husky was born in 1967 to honor Canada's centennial, then was refurbished in 1995 to rival the whales in Hudson's Bay. Lovingly built with a ton of steel and thirty-six sheets of plywood, this muskie greets guests along the Trans-Canada highway.

The largest fish sculpture in the world is a muskellunge, but it doesn't reside at the trademarked Musky Capital of the World (Boulder Junction, Wisconsin). Despite its title, that town has only a fishy painting on the side of a giant propane tank. Instead, the prize goes to Hayward, Wisconsin, with its 143-foot walk-through muskie, where lovers can exchange vows in the mouth of the fish.

This muskie towers over visitors to the Freshwater Fishing Hall of Fame in Hayward, Wisconsin. PHOTOGRAPH BY THE AUTHOR.

BASS AND TROUT

These two important fish may get overlooked by anglers, but a few loyal towns pay tribute. Ashland, Wisconsin, has a lively largemouth bass snagged by a red-and-white Lazy Ike. The seventeen-foot fish in Kalkaska, Michigan, leaps from the downtown fountain in honor of the state fish, the brook trout, and to remind visitors to attend the annual National Trout Festival in April. The southeastern Minnesota town of Preston keeps its trout mobile on the back of a trailer, lugging it to local festivals so the town can show off to its neighbors and lure tourists to its rivers.

The portable trout of Preston, Minnesota, works as a tourism promotional tool by making appearances in parades of neighboring towns, thanks to its handy mount on a trailer. PHOTOGRAPH BY THE AUTHOR.

THE WILY WALLEYE

Why are so many walleye statues called Willie, Willy, Wally, and even Captain Wylie? Just as many towns claim to be a fishing capital, these slippery names are deceptively similar. Both Garrison, Minnesota, and Garrison, North Dakota, claim to be a walleye capital with a nearly identical fish. One is named Wally Walleye and the other Wally the Walleye; you'll be excused if you mix them up. Originally the North Dakota walleye went by Willy, but the town backtracked when it learned that Baudette, Minnesota, had already named its pride Willie the Walleye. With a simple vowel movement, Garrison's walleye was named the more apt Wally the Walleye.

North Dakota's twenty-eight-foot fish took a beating from the weather and the birds that chose to make a nest in the poor fish's mouth. The fish in Gar-

Minnesota and North Dakota both have nearly identical walleyes in identically named towns (Garrison), and both claim to be a walleye capital. Here, Minnesota's Wally Walleye sports a new paint job after taking a beating from the wintry winds off Lake Mille Lacs. PHOTOGRAPH BY THE AUTHOR.

rison, Minnesota, also fell victim to harsh winds and needed special taxidermists to spruce him up. On a visit in autumn 2014, I saw Wally on a new stand overlooking Mille Lacs, and a hefty man assured his granddaughter, "Yeah, Suzy, Wally went to the hospital and he's all fixed up now. He's got all new fiberglass, so he's nice and shiny." The fish is a beacon to lost anglers on the giant lake, but they shouldn't

mistake him for a similar statue on the other side of the lake in the town of Isle.

The original giant walleye in Minnesota must be Baudette's 9,500-pound Willie the Walleye from 1959. This beefy beast helped the town secure its trademarked claim as the official Walleye Capital of the World, even if Port Clinton, Ohio, with its eighteen-foot walleye named Captain Wylie envies

The vicious teeth on this walleye near Ottertail Lake would surely scare kids. PHOTOGRAPH BY THE AUTHOR.

Just as early trick-photography postcards showed angling buckaroos atop bucking lunkers, Kabetogama, Minnesota, erected an advertising sign in 1949 that allowed tourists to prove that the bucking walleye phenomenon is not the stuff of legend.
PHOTOGRAPH BY THE AUTHOR.

the title. Many towns across the north woods boldly announce titles of "Capitals" and "World's Biggest," and no authority is set up to crack down on impostors; instead, they raise a giant fish to scare off the critics.

Despite these walleye wars, perhaps the best is not the biggest. In far northern Minnesota, Lake

Kabetogama claims the only equestrian walleye: a sixteen-foot concrete fish that sports a saddle for tourists to pop on for a snapshot. Originally part of an advertising sign when erected in 1949, the bucking walleye was hailed by sculptor Duane Beyers as the "World's Largest Walleye," a claim now easily surpassed. Other tourist traps have taken the bait

Slated to be demolished in 2013, the Beaver House in Grand Marais, Minnesota, has outfoxed the wrecking ball and is a landmark for visitors to Lake Superior's north shore. PHOTOGRAPH BY THE AUTHOR.

and offer similar rides/photo ops, such as the giant saddled sturgeon outside a cheese and fish shop in Prairie du Chien, Wisconsin.

The other truly original walleye crashes through the roof of Grand Marais's Beaver House, which began as a shoe repair shop but moved into the

212

Just shy of one ton (1,999 pounds, 15½ ounces), Paul Bunyan's walleye in Rush City, Minnesota, would make a tasty snack for the lumberjack. PHOTOGRAPH BY THE AUTHOR.

more lucrative fishing lure business. In the 1990s, artist Jim Korf added the flying fish, which threatens anyone entering the store with its enormous jowls hungry for customers.

Another menacing walleye weighs in at 1,999 pounds and looks ready to gobble pickups zooming along Interstate 35 in Rush City, Minnesota. This may not be the world's largest walleye, but this catch certainly would be a fine snack for Paul Bunyan. When I grilled the store manager about the "World's Largest" claim on its base, she quickly backpedaled, repeating, "It's just a joke. It's just a joke." The folks at Guinness haven't pulled out the measuring tape to monitor Rush City's catch, but the town still presents impressive fishing statistics to awe any angler: weight, 1,999 pounds, 15½ ounces; bait, thirty-five-pound tiger muskie; line, one-inch manila rope; rod, sixty-two-foot white pine; reel, three-ton logger's winch.

213

The sleek green muskie in Deer River, Minnesota, has been a part of this lake country resort community for as long as the locals can remember. PHOTOGRAPH BY THE AUTHOR.

NORTHERN PIKE

Paul Bunyan also battled Notorious Nate the Northern, but no one has raised a statue about it. As the tall tale goes, the ingenious lumberjack bred walleyes and northern pikes with lynx so the fish could grow fur coats to stave off Jack Frost during the infamous "year of two winters" when the mercury plummeted to record lows.

Despite northern pikes' ability to endure and thrive in chilly northern lakes, not many towns have statues in their honor compared to the wily walleye. Hope, Minnesota, has a twelve-foot chainsaw-sculpted northern pike with a giant Dardevle lure dangling out of its mouth.

Deer River, Minnesota, has a sleek northern pike that parents plop their kids on as though it's a cuddly pony. I asked the receptionist at the information desk

Overlooking beautiful Cameron Lake in Erskine, Minnesota, this bloodcurdling pike is eager for bait just about the size of some kids jumping off the dock. PHOTOGRAPH BY THE AUTHOR.

in the little tourist cabin for details about the pike next door. She turned down her television only long enough to reply, "Oh, I don't know. It's been around here as long as I can remember. Every town needs something, I guess." At least I knew that pesky park rangers wouldn't bother anyone climbing all over the sculpture to snap a photograph.

The best of the pike is in the northwestern Min-nesota town of Erskine, overlooking a sandy beach on pristine Cameron Lake. This menacing speckled fish provides the perfect photo opportunity for tourists: they can put their head in the mouth of the monster and imagine that such giant jaws waiting hungrily beneath the waves could take swimmers for bait. 🐟

A tranquil day's fishing awaits these two anglers as they venture on Whitefish Bay, Ontario, circa 1900–1910. PHOTOGRAPH BY DETROIT PUBLISHING COMPANY. LIBRARY OF CONGRESS PRINTS AND PHOTOGRAPHS DIVISION.

Gone Fishin'

Many men go fishing all of their lives without knowing that it is not fish they are after.

—Henry David Thoreau

Early tourism advertisements for the north woods boasted happy hunting and fishing grounds, and even now the area ranks first in the country in per capita sales of fishing licenses. Minnesota has one boat for every six residents and more than fourteen thousand lakes, with Wisconsin and Michigan close behind. The U.S. Census reported in 1991 that a million anglers spent $846,000,000 in Minnesota. By 2011, that number rose to a million and a half fishers with Minnesota licenses who spent almost $2,500,000,000. Across the United States, forty-six million Americans fish, and a third of them are women.

The sport is growing, but the strain on fish populations is acute despite conscientious fishers practicing catch and release. Consider that Minnesota's Department of Natural Resources lowered the limit on the state's most popular fishing spot, Lake Mille Lacs, to one walleye per angler per day in 2015, and then shut it down entirely before summer's end.

Medical research confirms what anglers have known for millennia: eating fish is healthy. Despite concern about mercury or other dangerous chemicals,

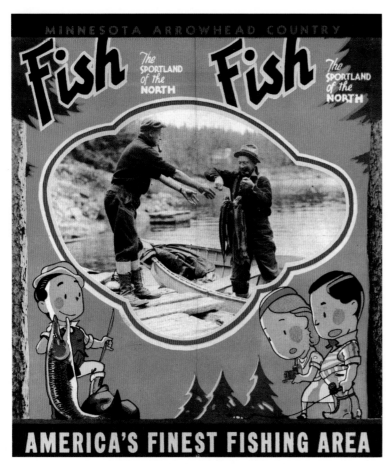

As recreational fishing became more profitable than commercial fishing in the north woods of Minnesota, tourism agencies began promoting the Arrowhead region to anglers near and far.

the Mayo Clinic reports that the benefits of two servings of fish per week outweigh other risks. Following this fishy regimen enhances your eyesight, increases brainpower, improves the skin, decreases problems of asthma, and can even raise men's sperm count. The longest-living people in the world inevitably reside along the waterfront—from Sardinia to Costa Rica to Japan.

Its benefit for diet misses the essence of why fishing is on the rise. In an age of ever-increasing speed with multiple forms of technology constantly vying for our attention, this sport forces us to detach and enjoy the sublime natural spectacle of the mist shrouding a northern lake at dawn as the rising sun struggles to break the spell. We are gently encouraged to be in the moment and remember that this is simply the best place to be. ❧

SELECTED BIBLIOGRAPHY

Abbot, J., ed. *Inside Cars.* New York: Princeton Architectural Press, 2001.

Aksakov, Sergei. *Notes on Fishing.* Evanston, Ill.: Northwestern University Press, 1997.

Breining, Greg. *Fishing Minnesota: Angling with the Experts in the Land of 10,000 Lakes.* Minneapolis: University of Minnesota Press, 2003.

Brown, Charles E. *Sea Serpents: Wisconsin Occurrences of These Weird Water Monsters.* Madison: Wisconsin Folklore Society, 1942.

Buckingham, Nash. *Blood Lines: Tales of Shooting and Fishing.* New York: Putnam, 1938.

Buffler, Rob, and Tom Dickson. *Fishing for Buffalo: A Guide to the Pursuit and Cuisine of Carp, Suckers, Eelpout, Gar, and Other Rough Fish.* Minneapolis: University of Minnesota Press, 2009.

Carter, Jimmy. *An Outdoor Journal.* New York: Bantam Books, 1988.

Carver, Jonathan. *Three Years Travels through the Interior Parts of North-America for more than Five Thousand Miles.* Philadelphia: Key and Simpson, 1796.

Chatham, Russell, ed. *Silent Seasons.* Livingston, Mont.: Clark City Press, 1988.

Cochrane, Timothy, and Hawk Tolson. *A Good Boat Speaks for Itself: Isle Royale Fishermen and Their Boats.* Minneapolis: University of Minnesota Press, 2002.

Coleman, Loren, and Patrick Huyghe. *The Field Guide to Lake Monsters, Sea Serpents, and Other Mystery Denizens of the Deep.* New York: Jeremy P. Tarcher/Penguin, 2003.

Colquhoun, Kate. *Taste: The Story of Britain through Its Cooking.* London: Bloomsbury, 2011.

Copley, Jon. "Fussy Fish Fake It." *New Scientist,* March 17, 2001.

Donne, John. *John Donne: The Major Works, including Songs and Sonnets and Sermons.* London: Oxford University Press, 2009.

Fagan, Brian M. *Fish on Friday: Feasting, Fasting, and the Discovery of the New World.* New York: Basic Books, 2006.

Fapso, Richard J. *Norwegians in Wisconsin.* Madison: State Historical Society of Wisconsin, 1977.

Fellegy, Joe. *Classic Minnesota Fishing Stories.* Minneapolis: Waldman House Press, 1982.

Garner, Shawn R., and Bryan D. Neff. "Alternative Male Reproductive Tactics Drive Asymmetrical Hybridization between Sunfishes." *Biology Letters,* November 13, 2013.

Godfrey, Linda S., and Richard D. Hendricks. *Weird Wisconsin*. New York: Barnes and Noble Books, 2005.

Godoy, Maria. "Lust, Lies, and Empire: The Fishy Tale behind Eating Fish on Friday." National Public Radio. npr.org. April 6, 2012.

Greenberg, Paul. *Four Fish: The Future of the Last Wild Food*. New York: Penguin, 2010.

Grover, Jan Zita. *Northern Waters*. St. Paul: Graywolf Press, 1999.

Hemingway, Ernest. *Hemingway on Fishing*. New York: Scribner, 2002.

Hoffbeck, Steven R. "'Without Careful Consideration': Why Carp Swim in Minnesota's Waters." *Minnesota History* 57, no. 6 (Summer 2001).

Hoover, Herbert. *Fishing for Fun and to Wash Your Soul*. New York: Random House, 1963.

Hughes, Robert. *A Jerk on One End: Reflections of a Mediocre Fisherman*. New York: Ballantine, 1999.

Irving, Washington. *Life of George Washington*. New York: G. P. Putnam, 1856.

Jones, Thelma. *Once upon a Lake*. Minneapolis: Ross and Haines, 1957.

Knapp, Rosemary, and Bryan D. Neff. "Steroid Hormones in Bluegill, a Species with Male Alternative Reproductive Tactics including Female Mimicry." *Biology Letters*, December 22, 2007.

Kortenhof, Kurt Daniel. *Long Live the Hodag: The Life and Legacy of Eugene Simeon Shepard, 1854–1923*. Rhinelander, Wis.: Hodag Press, 1996.

Legwold, Gary. *The Last Word on Lutefisk*. Minneapolis: Conrad Henry Press, 1996.

Lovoll, Odd. *The Promise of America*. Minneapolis: University of Minnesota Press, 1999.

Maclean, Norman. *A River Runs through It*. Chicago: University of Chicago Press, 2001.

McPhee, John. *The Founding Fish*. New York: Farrar, Straus and Giroux, 2002.

Meier, Peg. *Coffee Made Her Insane*. Minneapolis: Neighbors Publishing, 1988.

Norton, James. *Minnesota Lunch: From Pasties to Banh Mi*. St. Paul: Minnesota Historical Society Press, 2011.

Oppian of Cilicia. *Oppian, Collthus, Tryphiodorus*. New York: Putnam, 1928.

Peck, George W. *Peck's Fun*. Chicago: Belford, Clarke, 1882.

Plutarch. *Life of Antony*. Cambridge: Cambridge University Press, 1988.

Radcliffe, William. *Fishing from Earliest Times*. Charleston, S.C.: Nabu Press, 2010.

Roberts, Kate. *Minnesota 150: The People, Places, and Things That Shape Our State*. St. Paul: Minnesota Historical Society Press, 2007.

Rosenthal, Mike. *North American Freshwater Fishing*. New York: Scribner, 1989.

Rossow, Curt. *Some Just Get Away*. St. Cloud, Minn.: MK Publishing, 2006.

Saults, Dan, ed. *Sport Fishing USA*. Washington, D.C.: Bureau of Sport Fisheries and Wildlife, 1971.

Shapiro, Aaron. *The Lure of the North Woods: Cultivating Tourism in the Upper Midwest*. Minneapolis: University of Minnesota Press, 2013.

Sternberg, Dick. *The Art of Freshwater Fishing*. Minnetonka, Minn.: Cy DeCosse, Inc., 1982.

Thwaites, Reuben Gold, ed. *Travels and Explorations of the Jesuit Missionaries in New France*. Cleveland: Burrows Brothers, 1849.

Tufford, Julie Peterson. *Original Scandinavian Recipes*. Minneapolis: Julie Peterson Tufford Publishing, 1940.

Uehling, Thomas. *Minnesota's Angling Past*. Charleston, S.C.: Arcadia Press, 2013.

Walton, Izaak, and Charles Cotton. *The Compleat Angler*. Oxford: Clarendon Press, 1915.

Walker, Matt. *Fish That Fake Orgasms and Other Zoological Curiosities*. New York: St. Martin's Press, 2006.

Williams, Ted. *Something Fishy*. New York: Skyhorse Publishing, 2007.

Wurzer, Cathy. *Tales of the Road: Highway 61*. St. Paul: Minnesota Historical Society Press, 2008.

Zarchy, Harry. *Let's Fish*. New York: Alfred A. Knopf, 1960.

Zink, Robert M. *The Three-Minute Outdoorsman: Wild Science from Magnetic Deer to Mumbling Carp*. Minneapolis: University of Minnesota Press, 2014.

Eric Dregni is associate professor of English at Concordia University in St. Paul. He is the author of many books, including *Minnesota Marvels, Midwest Marvels, In Cod We Trust: Living the Norwegian Dream, Never Trust a Thin Cook and Other Lessons from Italy's Culinary Capital, Vikings in the Attic: In Search of Nordic America,* and *By the Waters of Minnetonka,* all published by the University of Minnesota Press. He lives in Minneapolis.